And the Church must be forever building, and always decaying, and always being restored.
—T. S. Eliot, *The Rock*

SPIRITUAL SPACE

THE RELIGIOUS ARCHITECTURE OF PIETRO BELLUSCHI

MEREDITH L. CLAUSEN

UNIVERSITY OF WASHINGTON PRESS

SEATTLE AND LONDON

Printed by C&C Offset Printing Co., Ltd., Hong Kong
Produced by Marquand Books, Inc.
Designed by Scott Hudson

The author gratefully acknowledges the contribution provided by an Arts and Humanities Research Professorship Grant from the Graduate School of the University of Washington.

Library of Congress Cataloging-in-Publication Data
Clausen, Meredith L.
    Spiritual space : the religious architecture of Pietro
  Belluschi / Meredith L. Clausen.
       p.   cm.
    Includes bibliographical references and index.
    ISBN 0-295-97213-0 (alk. paper)
    1. Church architecture—United States—Themes, motives.
  2. Synagogue architecture—United States—Themes, motives.
  3. Architecture, Modern—20th century—United States—
  Themes, motives. 4. Belluschi, Pietro, 1899–
  —Criticism and interpretation.   I. Title.
  NA5212.C57   1992
  726'.5'092—dc20   92-14621

Jacket: St. Mary's Cathedral, San Francisco (no. 26)
Back jacket: (left to right) Zion Lutheran Church, Portland, Oregon (no. 8); St. Margaret of Cortona Catholic Church, Columbus, Ohio (no. 27); First Presbyterian Church, Cottage Grove, Oregon (no. 11)
Frontispiece: Zion Lutheran Church, Portland, Oregon (no. 8)
Page 10: Pietro Belluschi, May 1972

CONTENTS

PREFACE

Pietro Belluschi has long awaited a book on his churches. Though this is not the book he would have written, I hope it accomplishes much the same end as the one he envisioned.

My work on Belluschi began with a different book, a monograph on his entire life and career, which is far larger in scope and more analytic in approach. As he and I, in the course of countless hours of taped interviews spanning the past seven or eight years, clashed over sticky issues faced in the earlier study, it occurred to me the situation would be eased by my first doing the book he wanted. This was a book, descriptive in approach and superbly illustrated, devoted to the churches and synagogues which in his mind constitute his most important body of work.

In this other book I tackle larger issues beyond the work itself, such as regionalism, changes in his modus operandi, the problem of collaboration and credit, and his role as adviser and adjudicator in the architectural profession at large. Belluschi's religious buildings make up only a fraction of his total body of work; to accomplish such an extensive oeuvre, Belluschi relied heavily on the contributions of others. His skill lay in recognizing the potential of an idea or strength of a form and drawing together the suggestions, design abilities, and accomplishments of others into something new, specifically geared to the problem at hand. Despite his modernist stance with its faith in novelty, Belluschi was not a form giver. If an existing solution made sense, he used it, regardless of its source. A deeply intelligent man, with a complex, penetrating mind, he was also equipped with a highly cultivated artistic eye. Whatever one thinks of his mode of practice or body of work as a whole, his refined, reticent churches with their understated elegance have unquestionably made a lasting contribution to modern church architecture.

In focusing on executed buildings or projects, the aim was to go beyond a simple descriptive catalogue of the works to the ideas behind them. In the introduction, I hope to give a sense of Belluschi's life and career while reserving a more thorough discussion for the other book, and to put his churches and synagogues in their social, historical, religious, and architectural contexts. The body of the text is devoted to the buildings themselves, sometimes simply describing them, sometimes expanding into longer essays to provide a fuller picture of what went into them—how Belluschi received the commission, his relations with the client, the nature of the design process—when it seemed germane. The intent was to provide as full a picture as possible of the climate of thought surrounding each work, addressing the question of how the building looks and why it looks that way, that is, what were the primary determinants of its form. Aware, too, of the insights gained from long conversations with Belluschi himself as well as from interviews with well over two hundred people he has worked with—members of his Portland office, associated architects, clients, and congregations—I hope that this information will be valuable to others in understanding his work. Some readers undoubtedly will find these sometimes anecdotal accounts irrelevant and will prefer just the basic facts. For them I have provided as many drawings, plans, sections, and photographs in each case as appropriate. My goal was to weave all this material— description of the buildings, brief sketch of Belluschi's career, his views on church architecture and how those views changed over time, and a sense of the general context in which he worked—into a dense web from which a clear pattern would emerge.

Belluschi would have liked a comprehensive survey of all the churches and synagogues in which he was involved. I chose instead to select only those I felt to be the most significant, and where his primary role in the design process was evident. As he was often called into projects as a kibitzer or design critic, it seemed to me more telling to concentrate on those in which his hand is clear. Yet it is sometimes difficult to determine who contributed how much of a design: with some projects Belluschi simply set the parameters in terms of site or client needs; with others he established the basic design concept, then turned the project over to associates for development and execution. I admit I may have erred in the selection even among those included here.

Belluschi's essays in the appendix, too, represent only a portion of those he wrote. He spoke often and wrote profusely, on a wide range of subjects for a wide range of audiences. He frequently repeated himself, referring back to earlier speeches either for ideas or in some cases actual text. Selected were essays that reveal the general climate of thought at the time or his specific aims and intentions. The aim was to offer the reader a clear picture of his ideas, in his own words, as they changed over time.

Dates typically indicate when the design process was begun and when the building was completed. More specific dates are given if the time lapse between the commission and the actual design and construction was longer than usual.

I owe gratitude to scores of people who, directly or indirectly, assisted in this work. To the librarians of the George Arents Research Library, Syracuse University, and the Oregon Historical Society in Portland; to Belluschi's collaborators and the associated architects who were good enough to take time to speak with me; to members of his congregations, the pastors, priests, and rabbis who willingly met with me; to all them and the many others who answered my letters and shared their thoughts, I give thanks. I would like to acknowledge in particular Jean Bony, professor and learned scholar of Gothic architecture at the University of California, Berkeley, whose penchant for clear thinking laid the foundations for my work; architect Henry Klein, a former member of Belluschi's Portland office and long-standing friend of Belluschi's who was kind enough to read the introduction; Mary Alice Hutchins, Frank Allen, and Walter Gordon, architects who also worked in Belluschi's office in the 1940s; Robert Brannen, of Jung/Brannen Associates, Inc., Boston, whose generous support counted in more ways than one; Mary Ellen Anderson and her aide Sarah Park for their help with legwork; Laura Burns Carroll and Pamela Perrin for their research assistance; and of course Marjorie Belluschi, without whose able hand any study of Belluschi would be incomplete. I would also like to extend gratitude to my editor Suzanne Kotz for her skillful assistance in clarifying my often tangled prose. Lastly, my thanks to family and friends for their tolerance and goodwill, and to my colleague Martha Kingsbury, who unwittingly lured me into all this.

INTRODUCTION

Great art is a dealing with simple subjects freshly.
—Alfred North Whitehead, *Dialogues of Alfred North Whitehead*

In the design of a church, Pietro Belluschi sought the meaning of the building rather than a compelling external form. Pursuing timeless rather than ephemeral values, he looked for the essence of the type rather than an innovative form whose interest would fade. His goal was to create an architecture appropriate to the modern age without destroying the symbols that had given meaning to the notion of "church" in the past.

Belluschi brought to sacred design his basic architectural tenets: rational structure, appropriate scale, harmonious proportions, fine materials and craftsmanship, subdued but dramatic light, and, most of all, eloquent, moving space. Belluschi strove to meet his congregation's unarticulated emotional wants as well as its purely practical demands. His ability to empathize, to sense what the congregation sought—whatever its denomination and particular liturgical requirements—gave him a profound understanding of its most fundamental needs.

Belluschi was born in 1899 in Ancona, a seaport on the Adriatic coast of Italy, and moved to Rome at the age of six; he was raised a Catholic and grew up steeped in the rituals of Roman Catholicism. From this experience he acquired both a fierce antipathy for institutionalized religion and an intuitive understanding of the factors that compose a spiritual space.[1] A sensitive, thoughtful, deeply intelligent man who early in life rejected unquestioned dogma, Belluschi in time came to see the power of the church building and its ability to generate spiritual feelings as residing in its appeal to the senses. The churches of his youth, among them Francesco Borromini's magnificent baroque St. Agnese in Rome, with their monumental domes, vast, sumptuously ornamented surfaces, interiors filled with music and the aroma of incense, and most of all their art—richly colored marbles and stained glass, gilded moldings, brilliant frescoes, and profuse sculptural decoration—aroused emotions and moved the spirit in a way that the more intellectualized, formal doctrines of the church could not. Recognizing the power of the traditional church, in his work Belluschi gave it new life by casting it in a freshly conceived modern form. In doing so, he rose above the limited and specific, the momentary needs and changing requirements of individual congregations, transcending denominational differences with the creation of compelling sacred spaces that appealed to believers and nonbelievers alike.

After receiving a degree in engineering from the University of Rome in 1922, Belluschi came to the United States on a one-year grant to study at Cornell University. There he earned a second degree, in civil engineering, and, instead of returning to Italy, remained in the United States, heading west in search of a job. After a short stint in a menial job in an Idaho mine, he moved to Portland, Oregon, in hopes of finding work with an architectural firm. In 1925 he joined the office of A. E. Doyle, one of the largest and most successful firms in Portland, known primarily for its high-quality commercial and institutional work. About the time Belluschi arrived, however, Doyle's health declined, and the office began to languish. The principal designer resigned late in 1927, and Doyle himself died shortly thereafter, leaving Belluschi, then only twenty-eight years old and without formal architectural training, in charge of design.

Struck almost immediately by a slumping economy, the office struggled to keep going during the lean years of the depression, coasting largely on the fame of the Doyle office and the recently finished,

Fig. 1. Morninglight Chapel, Finley Mortuary,
Portland, Oregon, 1936–37.

highly celebrated Portland Art Museum building, which Belluschi had designed as one of his first major projects in 1930.[2] In 1936, as the economy began to strengthen, the office was commissioned to design a new chapel for the Finley Mortuary in Portland, to be added to the existing 1912 Colonial Revival building. The old portions were also remodeled to unify the old and new parts (fig. 1, no. 1). Belluschi's building consisted of clean, simple, largely unornamented geometric blocks containing the new chapel, reception areas, administrative offices and other ancillary spaces, a simple colonnaded loggia, and a tall rectangular tower. True to Belluschi's modernist principles, the presence of the chapel was rationally expressed on the exterior, its semicircular apse rising above the projecting base of the building and lit by a continuous glass block clerestory that stopped just short of the apse. The exteriors of warm red brick were flush, defined simply by a thin limestone cornice but otherwise devoid of conventional moldings, dormers, and other historicizing projections. The flat or gently sloped roofs were without overhangs; weather protection was provided over walkways and the entrance by a simple portico.

The chapel, parabolic in plan with a traditional focus on the chancel end, was brilliantly lit with natural light from the clerestory reflected off the soft white ceiling and walls. An oculus in the apse created a strong directional pull and provided a dramatic focal point to the otherwise simply defined space. In this, his first church (called the Morninglight Chapel because of the flood of natural light it received in

the early hours), Belluschi established what was to remain a principal aim: creating a quiet, simple, spiritual space by the adroit use of light and minimal means. Destined for the city's culturally sophisticated upper classes, the Finley chapel was regarded as tasteful yet unpretentious.

The building was also seen as distinctly modern. Inspired by the crisp, clean, volumetric architecture of Scandinavian modernists such as Gunnar Asplund and Willem Dudok, and, less directly, contemporary Italian architects, the Morninglight Chapel rejected the traditional American colonial, Romanesque, or Gothic forms then in common use. Recognized by the American Institute of Architects for its modernity, the Finley chapel brought Belluschi national acclaim as the designer of one of the hundred most notable buildings constructed in the country since World War I.[3]

Belluschi's modernist principles were clear: rather than merely reproducing a historical prototype that no longer spoke a contemporary tongue, the architect, he believed, had to address each architectural problem anew. Imitating the Gothic church was inappropriate, as "practically all the living elements which then went into the creation of those older churches are now lacking—the honesty of construction and directness of expression, counterbalanced by the simplicity of their lives, the feeling for the materials at hand; the long training of the building crafts who [sic] had wonderful traditions of craftsmanship." All these were no longer part of modern life. The form might be imi-

Fig. 2. St. Thomas More Catholic Church, Portland, Oregon, 1939–40.

Fig. 3. St. Thomas More. Interior.

tated, but the spirit was gone. Rather than blindly copying the anachronistic forms of the past, the architect should try to recapture the essence of the type, with a simple, straightforward solution in tune with life as it is, in sympathy with local materials, the people, and the existing landscape.[4]

The small, low-cost Catholic church of St. Thomas More in the suburban hills west of Portland was designed in 1939 with these principles in mind (figs. 2, 3, no. 3). Modern in its simplicity and economy of means yet evocative of the traditional church, it was all but free of the historicizing elements both costly and contrary to progressive architectural principles. All the furnishings, including the baptismal font, altar, and pews, were designed by Belluschi himself or someone in the office under his supervision. Built by skilled local carpenters of Norwegian descent, with the fine craftsmanship, quiet elegance, and visual refinement for which Belluschi was quickly becoming known, the church affirmed the dual legacy of his urbane Italian background and the architectural sophistication of the Doyle firm.

St. Thomas More also bore the influence of Frank Lloyd Wright and the thriving Arts and Crafts tradition in the Pacific Northwest. Wright's work was by this time well known in the Portland area. The University of Oregon, under the leadership of Ellis Lawrence, dean of

the School of Architecture and Allied Arts, had more than a decade and a half earlier rejected the traditional Beaux-Arts curriculum in favor of a more organic approach. This meant conceiving the building as an organism adapted to and expressing the conditions of its particular environment. In 1922 Lawrence had brought W. R. B. Willcox, an alumnus of Adler and Sullivan's Chicago office, to head the department of architecture. Through Willcox and other advocates of Sullivan's theories in the Portland area, such as William Gray Purcell who had moved from the Midwest in 1920, the ideals of Sullivan and the Prairie School had spread, penetrating architectural practice in the city. The Doyle office, by the time Belluschi arrived in 1925, had already begun breaking from the historicizing tradition of McKim, Mead, and White in favor of Sullivan's more modern approach.[5]

Willcox also knew Frank Lloyd Wright, whose reputation spread in the late 1920s with his series of articles in *Architectural Record*, and was instrumental in inviting him to lecture at the University of Oregon in 1930. It was thus that Wright delivered the first of a series of celebrated talks published as the Kahn Lectures on Modern Architecture the following year. Belluschi obviously found Wright's theories compelling, no doubt especially moved by Wright's dedication of the published lectures to the "Young Men in Architecture," as he himself was

Fig. 4. A. E. Doyle, Wentz cottage, Neah-kanie, Oregon, 1916 (1989 photograph).

Fig. 5. Doyle, Wentz cottage. Interior.

then only thirty-one. He wrote to Wright for his support in persuading the Portland Art Museum trustees to accept his modern scheme for a new museum building.[6]

It was through his contacts at the museum, especially with the painter Harry Wentz, that Belluschi was exposed to Arts and Crafts ideals. Wentz was a faculty member at the Portland Art Museum and a long-standing friend of Doyle in whose downtown office building Wentz rented studio space. Belluschi studied drawing and watercolor with Wentz, and, after Doyle died, the charismatic painter became a mentor and one of Belluschi's closest friends. The two men spent holidays together hiking and sketching in the Oregon wilderness or vacationing at the small seaside cottage-studio Doyle had built for Wentz in 1916 (figs. 4, 5).

This small, unpretentious building proved to be pivotal in the formation of Belluschi's personal design ideals. Inspired by progressive turn-of-the-century architects in the San Francisco Bay Area such as Bernard Maybeck, whose work had been exhibited in the Portland Architectural Club shortly before Doyle began the cottage's design, the Wentz house-studio was a regional interpretation of Bay Area Arts and Crafts ideals. It appears likely that Maybeck's work in Berkeley served as its point of departure.[7]

Begun in Great Britain earlier in the nineteenth century and imported to California around the turn of the century, the Arts and Crafts movement called for a return to a preindustrial vernacular. In architecture, homes were to be built by skilled carpenters rather than by ma-

chine technology. The movement venerated handicrafts, and particularly objects designed by craftspeople dedicated to producing work both functional and beautiful. Furnishings and fixtures were to be handwrought rather than factory-made and store-bought, with an emphasis on quality design and execution and the use of straightforward, natural materials. Buildings and their furnishings were to be conceived with a general composition and color scheme that would ensure continuity in tone, texture, form, and character. Buildings were also to harmonize with the larger environment, to fit within the landscape as an integral part of the existing whole. Wood, especially unpainted and naturally weathered, was celebrated not only for its inherent beauty and its consonance with the landscape but for its economy. Above all, buildings were to be simple, with no applied ornament. Visual interest came from the design and craftsmanship of the structural members themselves—exposed rafters, roof timbers, modular wood framing. As Charles Keeler, spokesman for the small group of progressive Bay Area architects, wrote in *The Simple Home*: "Let the work be simple and genuine, with due regard to right proportion and harmony of color; let it be an individual expression of the life it is to environ, conceived with loving care for the uses of the family." Simplicity, significance, utility, and harmony were their watchwords.[8]

These principles governed the design of the Wentz cottage and, later, Belluschi's Church of St. Thomas More. Like the Wentz cottage, it had unpainted wood exteriors, a simple double-sloped pitched roof, banked windows, and exposed framing with revealed roof rafters on

Fig. 6. Artist's house in town (project), 1935.

Fig. 7. Antonin Raymond, St. Paul's Church, Karuizawa, Japan, 1934. Interior.

Fig. 8. Raymond, St. Paul's Church, scissor truss.

the interior, all handcrafted by local carpenters. Its domestic form, in keeping with the residential scale of the neighborhood, was drawn from a project for an artist's house in town that Belluschi had designed for Wentz in 1935 (fig. 6).[9]

St. Thomas More thus owed much to the American Arts and Crafts movement. But equally important in Belluschi's thinking was the influence of the Czechoslovakian architect Antonin Raymond. Raymond's modest Church of St. Paul in Karuizawa, Japan (see fig. 13), of unfinished cedar with exposed framing and a scissor truss over a longitudinal nave, published in the January 1935 *Architectural Record*, was a building that Belluschi, an avid reader of architectural magazines, obviously knew. Much of the detailing of St. Thomas More was evidently drawn from Raymond's work (figs. 7, 8). In March 1939, just as he began the design of the Portland church, Belluschi acquired Raymond's book, *Architectural Details*, which describes specific techniques of Japanese carpentry and woodwork.[10] It was only one of several books on Japanese design principles Belluschi was then studying, which introduced him to an architectural tradition that henceforth formed a major component of his own formal language.[11]

St. Thomas More was designed in 1939 and built the following year for less than the cost of a fine house. To the rest of the country,

still mired in a habit of building expensive, historicizing churches, the building provided an eloquent statement that a compelling spiritual space could be obtained by using the simplest of means. It was published in 1942 with several other buildings by Belluschi and played a major role in establishing him nationally as one of the major modern church designers in America.[12]

Modernism in the 1940s

During World War II, Portland was transformed into a major defense center with the growth of the Kaiser shipyards and other war-related industries on the Columbia River. Jobs for architects were nonetheless scarce, as wartime restrictions on materials brought all non-war-related construction to a halt. Belluschi, however, fared very well, in part because of his demonstrated ability to build quickly and cheaply, in part because of the extensive network of influential, well-to-do clients he had inherited from the Doyle firm. He was thus able to secure a lion's share of the government projects for war housing and shopping centers. In 1943 he acquired the Doyle practice and placed it under his own name. Thus, by the time the war ended, he, unlike other architects in the Portland area, had an intact operating office and was in a position to receive a large number of the jobs deferred during the war.[13]

Fig. 9. Church of the People (project), Seattle, 1945.

Fig. 10. Eliel Saarinen & Eero Saarinen, First Christian Church, Columbus, Indiana, 1942.

With the resumption of a peacetime economy in the mid-1940s, orthodox European modernism, embodying aims and formal values very different from those Belluschi had embraced before the war, had made significant inroads into the architecture of the Northwest.[14] Seeking a more progressive approach consistent with an increasing materialism and a growing reverence for objective, rational, scientific values, Belluschi turned to severe, unornamented, rectilinear forms. To lend them warmth, he used natural, textured materials, soft colored lighting, landscaping, and restrained, stylized art. Both the Church of the People (fig. 9, no. 5), a project Belluschi drew up for a site in Seattle, and the Central Lutheran Church in Eugene (no. 6) were conceived at this time. Bearing the influence of architects such as Eero Saarinen (fig. 10), their stark, volumetric forms, flat roofs, continuous ribbon windows, clean, unornamented brick surfaces, and flattened, stylized art marked a new direction in his work.

Such extreme modernism, however, was too much for most congregations. The postwar era saw momentous social change, including radically altered international relations, rapidly developing technology, an exploding population, shifting demographic patterns with large numbers of American families relocating in the suburbs, and a tremendous expansion of higher education, all of which affected the religious climate and the nature of church building. After an era of mounting secularism, religious leaders predicted a revival of religious values, as many Americans, disillusioned by the horrors of war and the equivocal results of modern science, rejected the progressive ideology pervasive in the prewar years that had provided so little spiritual assurance. Many turned back to the church and a tradition they trusted. Churches and synagogues, with their solid legacy of cultural, theological, and financial resources, provided comfort, a sense of rootedness, and continuity with the past. With the resurgence of faith evidenced by burgeoning congregations and bolstered by a flourishing economy, religious institutions throughout the country launched building programs long postponed, first by the depression, then by the war.

Yet in the wake of Auschwitz and Hiroshima, people simultaneously experienced a sense of foreboding and uncertainty. Americans were better educated, better read, and traveled more; decades of scientific progress had deeply eroded traditional religious beliefs. Religious leaders thus faced on the one hand a renewed desire for spiritual relief, and on the other a skepticism about accepted dogma and, indeed, the very nature of God. This dichotomy between a need for tradition and its reassurance and a demand for a new conception of religion befitting the modern era characterized the religious climate in the postwar years.[15] The tension forced such thoughtful architects as Belluschi to reconcile in physical form the demand for heritage and the expression of a fresh vision.

A related aspect of American postwar culture was the widespread appeal of the Far East. Many Americans, especially among the intelligentsia, no longer found the formal doctrines of Western religions credible and turned to Eastern thought for spiritual nourishment.[16] The personal, intuitive philosophies of China and Japan, very different from the rational, doctrinal approach of the West, provided convincing answers to persistent questions about the nature of God, the individual, and the relationship of self to the universe. What made this trend particularly germane to artists and architects was the centrality of aesthetics in Eastern thought.[17] In contrast to the West, where art served primarily as an instrument for conveying moral teachings, in the East art, or, more broadly, aesthetics, was seen as the source of religious thought, the very essence of spirituality. Tao was all-embracing, a continuous, undifferentiated, aesthetic whole that drew no distinction between self and God, self and others, self and nature. To act in accord with one's true nature was to act in harmony with the nature of all things. Aesthetics—the visual order of one's house, garden, indeed, one's own being—was thus evidence of an inner harmony and testimony to a universal order.

This pervasive interest in Eastern thought, with its reverence for simple things, the natural or "found" object as well as the man-made, and its search for an all-encompassing visual order, paralleled the architectural community's growing regard for Japanese architecture and landscape design. The formal qualities of Japanese architecture—simplicity, structural purity, spare, elemental form and elegance obtained by an utmost economy of means—resonated not only in the architecture of Frank Lloyd Wright, whose influence in the United States was by this time widespread, but also in the work of Mies van der Rohe. For religious buildings, the Japanese approach appealed because of its spiritual dimension. As Belluschi later put it, "Architecture was always related to the environment, always related to the trees, the rocks. It was a great lesson we learned from the Japanese."[18]

Religious attitudes changed in the postwar era, but so did the operational requirements that religious institutions were asked to meet.

While the buildings remained primarily places for common worship, the nonreligious social role expanded into highly organized community centers.[19] Architects were asked to provide not only new and larger sanctuaries for burgeoning suburban families but a wide variety of other building types as well—Sunday schools, fellowship halls, auditoriums, kitchens, nursery rooms, even athletic facilities. Site planning, in addition to design, thus became an increasingly important skill for the church architect.[20] This development can easily be seen in Belluschi's church plans, which began with the simple rectangular sanctuary of St. Thomas More (no. 3) in the late 1930s and expanded to a vast site-filling complex of interlocking multifunctional buildings for the Church of the Redeemer (no. 17) in the mid-1950s.

But, according to the modernist creed, as functions changed, so too should forms. Belluschi at this time had little hope that modern architecture could satisfy spiritual needs. In his essay "An Architect's Challenge," published in 1949 in *Architectural Forum* (Appendix), Belluschi pointed out that in society's quest for scientific progress, emotional expression was being lost. Painters and poets turned to hermetic introspection; sculptors were no longer interested in integrating their work with the surroundings; architects seemed incapable of building monumental buildings with emotional power. Missing was a sense of inner conviction. And of all creative endeavors, the church building, he felt, showed most clearly the loss of spiritual values. Yet to many, "God is still an intimate necessity; [people are] not satisfied by the knowledge that social advances have been made." Modern religious establishments were failing, as the design of their churches made clear.

Yet, according to Belluschi, architects who had rejected the obsolete forms of the past were finding it difficult to come up with new ones. In effect, what the architect was being called on to articulate, or give visual form to, was a set of religious beliefs that were inchoate and still evolving. What *was* the religious vision of the twentieth century the architect was being asked to express? Only by carefully listening to each individual congregation was Belluschi able to conceive what he felt was an appropriate answer.

Belluschi contrasted modern life to that of the Middle Ages, when the whole community had revolved around the church. He concluded his 1949 essay on the design of the modern church by suggesting that

Fig. 11. Zion Lutheran Church, Portland, Oregon, 1948–50.

Fig. 12. Gunnar Asplund, Woodland Chapel, Stockholm, 1918–20.

Fig. 13. Antonin Raymond, St. Paul's Church, Karuizawa, Japan, 1934.

given the times small buildings for communal gatherings, scaled to humans rather than to God, were more appropriate than monumental cathedrals. As he saw it, the challenge for the architect lay not in erecting great monuments but in creating intimate spaces conducive to spiritual thought.

Belluschi's churches of the later 1940s marked his struggle to find a form that lived up to his principles of modern architecture yet recalled enough of tradition to bespeak "church." Congregations still wanted buildings that looked churchlike, with all the recognizability and familiarity of the traditional type. Belluschi's solution was to take a known form and purify it, reducing it to its basic elements, which he then reinterpreted in modern terms.

Such a solution appeared in the Zion Lutheran Church in Portland (fig. 11, no. 8). Nordic in character, the church was appropriate for its conservative Lutheran congregation. The building is traditional in plan but wholly modern in its structural system. The great gabled roof is supported by an internal, exposed freestanding framework of pointed laminated arches enclosed by insulating, non-loadbearing brick cavity walls. With its hipped front over the narthex supported by a simple colonnade, Zion Lutheran suggests the influence of Gunnar Asplund's Woodland Chapel in Stockholm (fig. 12) but more likely was inspired by Antonin Raymond's St. Paul's Church in Karuizawa, Japan

(fig. 13). A simple slender spire rises above a tapered square base, like that of Raymond's church, finessing in the Belluschi church the awkward juncture of narthex and nave. To relieve the overall plainness of the form, Belluschi sheathed the portal, the traditional symbolic gate to heaven, with a copper bas-relief of abstracted hovering angels.

With its simple, dominant pyramidal roof brought down low to form a portico and internally exposed freestanding laminated arch structural system, Zion Lutheran introduced a concept Belluschi was to return to repeatedly in his later work. It occurs again, for example, in the 1959 Episcopalian church in Concord, Massachusetts, where the connection with Asplund's work seems even more apparent (no. 18), and still later, in another variant, in the University of Portland Chapel in 1985 (no. 38).

St. Philip Neri, whose Catholic congregation of largely Italian origin wanted a building recalling the simple basilican churches of their native land, represented a very different solution (fig. 14, no. 10). With the Early Christian basilica in mind, but also Saarinen's recent work such as the Lutheran church in Minneapolis with its simple, bold, geometric forms, rough-textured brick exterior, and gently pleated nave wall (fig. 15), Belluschi designed a plain, large-scale brick building, rectangular in plan, with a high-ceilinged axial space focused on the altar. The nave, defined by plain white plaster walls, is covered by an

Fig. 14. St. Philip Neri Catholic Church, Portland, Oregon, 1946–52. Interior.

Fig. 15. Saarinen, Saarinen & Associates. Christ Church Lutheran, Minneapolis, 1950. Interior.

Fig. 16. Central Lutheran Church, Portland, Oregon, 1948–50.

Fig. 17. Curved gateway, Nara Club, Nara, Japan.

exposed trussed timber roof, as in the Early Christian church. Unlike Zion Lutheran, St. Philip Neri was designed for Catholic pageantry and the clerical performance of a mysterious rite. The chancel is thus somewhat more richly adorned, with the altar and crucifix set off from the nave by a high, stepped platform and framed by an arching gilded wooden baldachino.

For the more affluent, culturally sophisticated congregation of the Central Lutheran Church of Portland (fig. 16, no. 9), the form was more distinctly modern, suggesting the influence of both Alvar Aalto, with its simple blank-walled curved apse and richly textured brick, and the Japanese, with its open timber framework, modular system, and curved-roof gate. Belluschi had admired Aalto's work, especially his use of wood in the Finnish Pavilion at the 1939 New York World's Fair, which he saw as validating his own growing interest in the natural material. Like that of the Japanese, Aalto's work offered viable solutions to many of the problems architects were beginning to face in the Pacific Northwest.[21] The unmistakably Japanese quotations in Central Lutheran, such as the sheltered gateway with its upturned eaves, appear to have been drawn from books such as Jiro Harada's *The Lesson of Japanese Architecture* (1936; fig. 17) or Samuel Newsom's *Japanese Garden Construction* (1939), both acquired by Belluschi in the late 1930s, when he was studying the work of Antonin Raymond.[22] Bellu-

schi's exposure to the more philosophical aspects of Eastern thought, particularly Zen Buddhism, was to come later, after he moved to the East Coast in 1951 to assume the deanship at MIT.

Belluschi's efforts to find an appropriate contemporary form that met his congregation's specific spiritual needs were resolved in one of his finest achievements of the period, the First Presbyterian Church in the small town of Cottage Grove, Oregon, in 1948 (fig. 18, no. 11). For all its evident analogies with both Aalto and the Japanese, it marked a very personal interpretation of modernism.

Representing a clear break with Catholicism, the Presbyterian faith tends to stress social values over otherworldly ones; the Cottage Grove Presbyterian in particular was known for its sense of social responsibility and responsiveness to the local community. The unpretentious, low horizontal forms and gently undulating roofline, breaking away from a more traditional soaring vertical one; the domestic scale in keeping with the small, wood-frame houses of the neighborhood; and the use of warm, textured, unpainted wood (locally cut and the principal source of the town's economy) aptly express community involvement[23] and represent a culmination of Belluschi's humanistic, regional approach to modern architectural design.

Fitting into its wooded surroundings, sited to preserve the existing trees, and focused inward on a private, secluded garden, First Presby-

Fig. 18. First Presbyterian Church, Cottage Grove, Oregon, 1948–51.

Fig. 19. Great rock, First Presbyterian Church (1989 photograph).

terian expresses, too, the harmony of the individual and nature, one's part in the larger whole. The great rock at the entrance, quarried and hauled to the site by the parishioners, while serving to screen the glazed sanctuary from public view, adds a touch of the "found" or seemingly fortuitous (fig. 19). Combined with the wholly rationalized structure of the building itself, it serves as an expression of a Zen principle: the harmony of the cultivated and spontaneous. The utter simplicity of the building, its sense of repose, and its oneness with nature express architecturally not only the liturgical demands of the congregation but the spiritual ideal of universal harmony at the core of Eastern thought. The church marks a climax in Belluschi's search for a moving, spiritual space, fully modern and appropriate to its time and place.

The 1950s: Belluschi in the East

In January 1951 Belluschi moved to Cambridge, Massachusetts, to assume the deanship of architecture and urban planning at MIT. By this time he was one of the most highly respected figures in his field. His technologically progressive, aluminum-sheathed Equitable Building in Portland, completed in 1948, as well as his much admired simple regional houses and churches in the Pacific Northwest, had brought him to the forefront of the profession.

With the move east, Belluschi's modus operandi changed. In Portland, he had had his own office, which he operated on an informal, openly collaborative basis, seeing himself primarily as a catalyst for design, encouraging and stimulating the ideas of others. Typically he would establish the basic concept of a project, then turn it over to others to develop and carry out. Belluschi, however, remained ultimately responsible for the final design solution. He also handled all client negotiations, especially for church commissions. Although these jobs rarely brought profit, they provided him an outlet for artistic expression; he relished them, as they offered relief from his more taxing projects and yielded far more personal satisfaction.

In assuming full-time responsibilities as dean at MIT, Belluschi gave up his office and henceforth practiced architecture independently, as a design consultant—sometimes as design architect, often more as a design critic—in association with other firms. The Portland office was sold to Skidmore, Owings & Merrill, which continued to operate it under the name of Belluschi/Skidmore, Owings & Merrill until projects begun under his direction were completed.[24] By now Belluschi was at the height of his fame, known throughout the world as a leading modernist and designer of churches. Not surprisingly, his first commissions in the East were for religious buildings, mostly around Boston.

Belluschi was also well known as a compelling speaker. As such, he was repeatedly asked to address issues relating to the controversy in

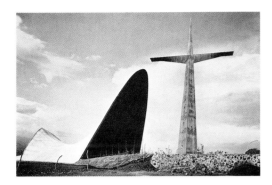

Fig. 20. Felix Candela, Chapel of Las
Lomas, Cuernavaca, Mexico, 1958–59.

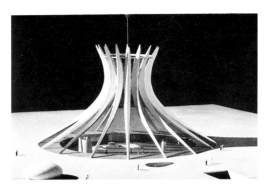

Fig. 21. Oscar Niemeyer, Crown of Thorns
Chapel, Brasília, Brazil, 1957–64.

Fig. 22. Antonin Raymond, Priory of
St. Anselm, Tokyo, 1955.

church design. The debate revolved principally around two issues: the question of style—whether a modern or traditional approach was more appropriate for contemporary church buildings—and the ramifications of liturgical reform on church planning.

The liturgical reform movement, calling for a fundamental rethinking of the Catholic liturgy, had begun in Europe just before World War I and over several decades gradually expanded in breadth and influence to other denominations as well.[25] The movement remained limited in the United States, despite the sponsorship of the Benedictine order, until the Second Vatican Council convening in 1963 mandated the reforms. Congregational passivity in the performance of the liturgy which had developed over the centuries demanded change. What had been a communal act in the Early Christian community became removed during the Middle Ages, both figuratively and literally, to the hands of the priests, who performed the eucharist as a mysterious rite on behalf of the people. The role of the congregation was thus reduced to one of spectatorship. Liturgically the distance was symbolized in the continued use of Latin, which few worshipers understood. Architecturally the separation was expressed by and perpetuated in the traditional longitudinal plan, with its nave, or congregational space, discrete from and visually focusing on the stagelike raised space of the altar in the chancel. In the course of twentieth-century reform, the liturgy was revamped to bring the laity back as active participants in the worship service, and the traditional rectangular plan was rejected in favor of a centralized plan that would reunite the congregation spatially with the liturgical center.

As the demand rose for new churches to accommodate the reforms, a floodgate was opened to modern architects eagerly seeking opportunities to explore new architectural directions. Experimentation was rampant and often wild, as progressive architects, equipped with structural techniques developed between the wars using steel and reinforced concrete, pursued a wide range of forms—circular, starshaped, elliptical, trapezoidal, parabolic—all ostensibly aimed at bringing the congregation as close to the liturgical center as possible. Especially in South America and Mexico, where labor was cheap and building restrictions were less stringent than in the United States, architects such as Felix Candela (fig. 20) and Oscar Niemeyer (fig. 21) fully exploited the potential of new structural technology. Their work paralleled that of Raymond and Rado in Japan (fig. 22), Pier Luigi Nervi in Italy, Eduardo Torroja in Spain, Kenzo Tange in Japan, Marcel Breuer in the United States (fig. 23), and of course Le Corbusier in France (fig. 24), with innovative, free-flowing sculptural buildings in slab and thinshell concrete.

Much of the work bordered on structural exhibitionism, as architects all too often regarded new church commissions as opportunities to create novel, eye-catching forms rather than the kind of spiritual

21

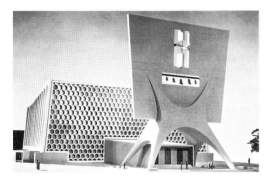

Fig. 23. Marcel Breuer, St. John's Abbey, Collegeville, Minnesota, 1960.

Fig. 24. Le Corbusier, Ronchamp Chapel, France, 1950–55.

Fig. 25. Belluschi and MIT students, 1956.

spaces demanded by liturgical reforms. Belluschi recognized this danger and cautioned against the pursuit of stylistic concerns for their own sake. "Architectural forms which are not born of logic, study and deep understanding of the peculiar problems at hand but come out of preconceived aesthetic theories," he wrote in *Architectural Record*, "will always be in danger of becoming artificial, tricky, or just fashionable."[26]

To most architects in the United States, however, the issue of liturgical reform and its implications for church planning was of less concern than the question of style. What had been a mere trickle of interest in modernism before the war was now widespread. As its influence grew, the dilemma modernism posed for church architects—whether to embrace or oppose it—became urgent. The decade of the 1950s saw the biggest growth in church building the nation had ever experienced; of marginal interest to the architectural profession earlier in the century, the church, responding to the resurgence of interest in religion among Americans, now became one of the most important building types of the decade. An article in *Nation's Business* reported that in the first half of the decade alone Americans spent more than $3 billion on religious architecture—churches, cathedrals, chapels, temples, synagogues, and other houses of worship. Churches, now ranked the fourth largest category of private construction, composed a major portion of the building industry's prosperity.[27] The vast majority of these buildings were, however, even in the 1950s, still being built in a traditional style.

The article, illustrated by a photograph of Belluschi discussing several new churches with students at MIT (fig. 25), focused on the revolution in church design. Whereas a decade before, most new churches were traditional, now, the article pointed out, more than 10 percent of new ones were expected to be "of boldly modern design." It was clear, however, that modernism was still facing opposition, as attested by the outcry over Skidmore, Owings & Merrill's sleek tubular steel and aluminum design for the Air Force Academy Chapel in Colorado Springs, on which Belluschi had been brought in as adviser.[28]

Similar articles on new developments in church architecture were regularly featured throughout the 1950s in general publications such as *Time*, *Life*, and the *New York Times*. The church was also a regular subject of building-type studies in architectural magazines and was frequently the focus of international symposia, with participants drawn from the fields of theology and philosophy as well as architecture. Belluschi was almost invariably involved.

The issue was important enough to be the subject of an American Institute of Architects symposium at the organization's 1950 annual national convention.[29] Belluschi was one of six panelists. For him, designing the religious building meant facing "the difficult problem of creating form appropriate to a modern society without destroying the many symbols which have given formal validity to the idea of a *church* in the past." What was important was maintaining "that feeling of emotional continuity which is the very essence of religion." This emotional continuity, Belluschi believed, could not be provided simply by good design. Notions of what constituted good design, like beauty, changed over time. The task of the creative architect was to seek something more, to go beyond "good design" to provide emotional depth.

Belluschi was posing a typological problem: how to cast a traditional form in modern terms without losing the richness of meaning and associations of the original type. Committed modernist that he was, he nonetheless defended tradition in church design, not its outdated exterior form but its rich heritage of symbols and associations which, in the late 1940s and early 1950s, was being rejected by the more orthodox European modernists dominating East Coast academia. Outwardly contemptuous of Belluschi's humanistic, regional approach, they considered it "soft," lacking intellectual rigor.[30] It was against this rigorous European modernism and its unilateral, doctrinaire rejection of history, which effectively cut architecture off from the past, that the postmodernists, galvanized by Robert Venturi, were to rebel a decade later; they demanded a return to history, meaning, and the richness of association.

Four years later, in 1954, Belluschi addressed the same issue of modern versus traditional to a broader audience in the *New York Times Magazine*:

> To many people the word "modern" is still synonymous with "barren," and lacking in the spiritual richness, the subtle emotional qualities, which sustained the great styles of the past. They complain that there is no "beauty" in modern architecture, as if beauty were a quality forever embalmed in time rather than forever changing, even as life is changing. They fail to see that the best architects of our age are, in fact, attempting to do just what creative architects of all times have always done, that is, to impart spiritual significance to the forms they are creating, and that it is their way to search for a deeper meaning of beauty. ("The Modern Church—or Traditional?" Appendix)

In referring elsewhere to the creative powers of the architect as "truly a divine gift," Belluschi reflected the general climate of the time. The late 1940s and 1950s saw the glorification of the architect as a cultural hero. Driven by the media, Americans became infatuated with the romantic image of the architect as the misunderstood, alienated creative genius committed solely to the integrity of his artistic vision. Frank Lloyd Wright, whose stature as a national hero by this time rivaled that of the great European architects Le Corbusier, Mies van der Rohe, and Walter Gropius, was widely cultivated as a role model, providing the point of departure for Ayn Rand's best-selling novel, *The Fountainhead*. Published in 1943, the book was made into a movie starring Gary Cooper in 1949, adding sex, glamour, and machismo to the image of the architect.

Popular magazines such as *Time* added momentum to the trend, celebrating in cover photographs and feature articles star architects such as Edward Durell Stone, Eero Saarinen, and Philip Johnson. The impact of this reverence for the arrogant creative genius, especially on the young, was widespread. Scores of starry-eyed young men, inspired by the *Fountainhead* image, were led to architecture as a profession. Architectural schools especially were affected, as students, awestruck by the celebrated architect, turned away from their stodgy professors to follow the design trends of the latest star. The reverence for the self-contained, isolated architect, whose work was governed by his artistic ideals alone, was sanctioned by Irving Stone's best-selling novel *The Agony and the Ecstasy*, a fictionalized account of Michelangelo's heroic struggle to rebuild St. Peter's in Rome. The book was published in the early 1960s, just as Belluschi was embarking on the design of St. Mary's Cathedral in San Francisco. The analogy was clear.

On a more profound level, Belluschi's statement on the divine gift of the creative artist reflected his own absorption in the writings of the mathematician and philosopher Alfred North Whitehead, whose work he encountered shortly after arriving at MIT.[31] Whitehead had attempted to formulate a coherent philosophy of life that would integrate the various components of the factional modern world—the objective data from mathematics and natural and social sciences, as well as subjective religious, moral, and aesthetic experience. His aim was to provide a single, logical body of thought that would serve as a guide for civilized living.

Though Whitehead was widely criticized for his often tentative, undeveloped ideas and abstruse language, Belluschi found convincing his efforts to rise above the prevailing emphasis on the hard sciences with a broader, more humanistic approach that recognized and accepted certain unknowns. Belluschi found particularly cogent Whitehead's insights into the nature of religion and his personal definition of God. As Whitehead described it, religion was an attempt to explain the relationship between human beings and the universe. Though beyond understanding, it could not be disregarded, as religious faith was needed by all thoughtful people, even scientists. In a passage Belluschi felt to be particularly compelling, Whitehead defined religion as "the vision of something which stands beyond, behind, and within, the passing flux of immediate things; something which is real, and yet waiting to be realized; something that gives meaning to all that passes, and yet eludes apprehension; . . . The worship of God is not a rule of safety—it is an adventure of the spirit, a flight after the unattainable."[32]

Belluschi first encountered Whitehead through a series of essays published in the *Atlantic Monthly* in 1954 and then went on to read the just-published *Dialogues of Alfred North Whitehead*.[33] Affected deeply by Whitehead's insights, he referred to him often, quoting him at length, for example, in his talk at the 1957 national convention of the American Institute of Architects in Washington, D.C.[34] He saw Whitehead as someone able to address basic questions of life while also respecting the modern scientific bent of mind, as a kindred spirit who conceived of the artist as a seeker of truth, the discoverer of a higher reality beyond the self. Envisioning both art and religion as a search for truth, Whitehead provided Belluschi a way of reconciling his own spiritual concerns with his work as an architect, of rationally understanding his role as a creative being in the larger realm.[35]

Whitehead perceived the creative spirit as a dynamic source of infinite possibilities, always changing because life and the process of reality were in constant change. The artist brought to light what others did not see, revealing an aspect of reality unknown before. Thus the artist was not just an enhancer of the known but a discoverer of the unknown, not just a priest but a prophet.[36] As Belluschi interpreted Whitehead's philosophy, this creative desire to seek a higher truth was what drove the artistic process, compelling the architect to find new forms and new solutions, to contribute to and become part of continuously changing, emerging reality.

Belluschi defended modernism in church architecture by pointing out that people needed more from religion than just a moral code. If society expected the church to meet spiritual as well as doctrinal needs, it would require a church building that spoke to the emotions. And such a building, he maintained, could come about only through a freshly conceived form, not a derivative one, since the latter no longer spoke in compelling terms.

In defining the main function of the church building as providing emotional fulfillment, creating "an environment in which the average man may find spiritual shelter," Belluschi made clear a fundamental difference between his work and Mies's. Mies's chapel on the Illinois Institute of Technology campus in Chicago (fig. 26) was a rational, perfectly designed structural jewel. Universal in form and space, it represented to many people, however, the emotional aridity they felt to be characteristic of modern architecture. By contrast, Belluschi's First Presbyterian Church in Cottage Grove (see fig. 18) was specific, its form sanctioned by tradition, its space determined by its spiritual purpose, unique to the particular moment and place.

Whitehead influenced much of Belluschi's thinking, but so too did the theologian Paul Tillich. Belluschi came to know of Tillich's philosophy in 1955 at a symposium sponsored by *Architectural Forum* on theology and architecture, which focused on the nature of the church and its purpose in contemporary society. Moderated by Douglas Haskell, the editor of the magazine, the symposium included as participants Belluschi; Dean Darby Betts, Cathedral of St. John, Providence, Rhode Island; the Reverend Marvin Halverson of the National Council of Churches; the architect and churchman Albert Christ-Janer; and the architect Morris Ketchum of Ketchum, Gina and Sharp. Paul Tillich, of the Harvard Divinity School, was the keynote speaker (fig. 27).[37]

In his writings, Tillich defined religion broadly as a feeling or state of mind rather than an institution or formal doctrine. Describing it simply as "a state of being driven by ultimate concerns," he saw it as something present in all spiritual life. All creative endeavors, even those not overtly religious, were religious in nature to the degree that they expressed something of a deeper level of reality, or what he called an ultimate concern.[38]

Fig. 26. Mies van der Rohe, chapel at Illinois Institute of Technology, Chicago, 1952.

Fig. 27. Theology and Architecture Symposium sponsored by *Architectural Forum* (Paul Tillich, head of table; Belluschi, third from left).

Aesthetics played a vital role in Tillich's theology. He believed the visual arts were able to arouse emotions and create experiences not communicable in words, to impart values beyond those of the rational, scientific, materialistic world. It was thus through art that the church expressed these values uncommunicable by other means.[39] Art was religious not by virtue of any particular style or subject matter but rather by its ability to convey the artist's personal vision of reality. Picasso's *Guernica*, Tillich felt, was one of the greatest religious paintings of the twentieth century, not because of its overt imagery but because of its underlying emotions, its spiritual dimension.[40] Rejecting traditional religious art as lacking emotional power and no longer capable of conveying meaning, Tillich endorsed modern art, particularly expressionism, whose nonfigurative, expressive power was able to convey the required emotional depth. He found nonrepresentational stained glass appropriate for contemporary society and the modern church, as it was free from worn-out, meaningless symbols and instead created an abstract "mystical light."[41] Formulating what he called a theology of art, he maintained that through the medium of art—painting, sculpture, and architecture—divine nature, or God, was revealed.

Tillich believed that the church building was one of the few religious symbols that still had power to convey something of the reality for which it stood. The meaning of much of the traditional symbolism of architectural forms of the past—the magnificent monumental masonry domes, towering west fronts, and soaring spires of traditional Gothic and baroque churches—had been lost through the ages. New, modern church buildings, rejecting such worn-out symbolism in favor of forms derived from considerations of function or structure, became in themselves symbols, embracing contemporary values and, at their best, conveying spiritual significance in a way few other creative endeavors did. Arguing against the imitative use of traditional historical types with their obsolete symbolism and costly adornments that cluttered space without conveying meaning, Tillich felt that religious integrity, hence beauty, derived from the usefulness and expressive power of the structure itself. Novelty for its own sake, however, was dishonest and especially inappropriate in a church, where moral content must be apparent. The architect's aim should be to provide a spiritual dimension, arouse an awareness of a higher level of reality, and create an environment conducive to a personal revelatory experience, not just to manipulate form.[42]

In another address to the American Institute of Architects at its 1957 national convention, Tillich spoke specifically of space. Tillich had defined "environment" as that portion of the individual's surroundings that held personal significance. This environment or space, however, was limited. Limited space protected and reassured, but, because it confined and restricted, it also produced anxiety. Infinite space, in contradistinction, was both liberating and threatening, opening up an

Fig. 28. First Lutheran Church, Boston,
1955–57 (1987 photograph).

endless realm of possibilities but poised to overwhelm the individual in its empty vastness. The individual needed both: limited space in which to feel both psychologically and physically protected, and infinite space for a sense of unendingness, with all its potential.[43] An interior space, such as that of a church, represented a finite portion of the infinite, a limited space protected and sheltered yet suggestive of the unlimited universal space of which it formed a part. The church interior, Tillich felt, should thus be both enclosed and open, a space both psychologically comforting and spiritually uplifting.

The ability of space to provide both privacy and a sense of communion with others was of particular importance in church design. Even amid others in common worship, the individual needed psychological space for private devotion. Tillich saw the church as a place providing spiritual shelter, where personal revelatory experiences could occur, a place where people felt "able to contemplate the holy in the midst of their secular life."[44] Tillich thus conceived of architecture, as did Belluschi, not as form but as space.

Tillich's concept of "holy emptiness," expressed architecturally in the interior of the modern church,[45] held particular meaning for Belluschi, who was wrestling with such questions as how the architect was to convey a sense of holiness and to express architecturally a spiritual presence without resorting to traditional symbols. Tillich suggested an answer with his concept. Holy emptiness was quite different from merely an empty church where one felt something was missing; rather, it was a meaningful emptiness where one sensed a deeper, broader dimension, a space filled with the presence of something that could not be expressed in any finite form.[46]

The accordance Belluschi felt with Tillich's theories was mutual. The concept of holy emptiness, Tillich maintained, was not a hypothetical ideal but one that could be found in the modern church. As proof he cited the Cottage Grove Presbyterian Church. Tillich said on visiting it in 1956, "This church restores my faith that modern architecture can be numinous."[47]

Churches and Synagogues of the 1950s

Belluschi's first religious building in the East was the First Lutheran Church of Boston (fig. 28, no. 12). Commissioned in 1954 for a cramped corner site in the Back Bay, it was traditional in plan, with a simple rectangular nave. Belluschi now included as part of the scheme a small, private garden through which one progressed before entering the church. The parti of a sheltered entrance and landscaped garden as an inherent part of the church, introduced in the Cottage Grove Presbyterian to provide a transition between the secular life of the street and the spiritual life of the church, remained henceforth a constant in Belluschi's religious buildings. The progression through space and the sense of expectation were to Belluschi subtle but essential elements in the experience of architecture. The thin, lightweight curved concrete slab roof, poised on steel columns embedded in and extending above the plain brick exterior walls, drew on developing technology in shell

Fig. 29. Portsmouth Abbey Church, Portsmouth, Rhode Island, 1957–61 (1987 photograph).

Fig. 30. Church of San Vitale, Ravenna, Italy, 526–47.

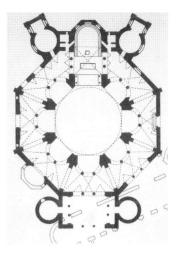

Fig. 31. Church of San Vitale. Plan.

structures. Because of the scheme's efficient use of materials, it proved an appropriate solution for the restricted budget and tightly constricted, marshy site. Though technically a departure in Belluschi's work and attesting his continuing exploration of new structural systems, the rational structure, quiet meditative interior, and progression of spaces were all continuations of Belluschi's earlier concerns.

The Portsmouth Abbey Church for a Benedictine monastery on a spacious semirural site in Rhode Island pursued a very different design direction (fig. 29, no. 13). The Benedictine order, known for its progressive attitude toward the fine arts, had demonstrated its support of modern architecture with buildings such as Raymond and Rado's concrete folded-slab Priory of St. Anselm in Tokyo (see fig. 22) and Marcel Breuer's highly sculptural St. John's Abbey in Minnesota (see fig. 23). Not surprisingly, given the abbey's concern to find a distinctly modern architect whose work would harmonize with the rural landscape, the Portsmouth fathers turned to Belluschi rather than to a more formalistic architect or to an architect with the austerity of orthodox European modernism.[48]

As the primary sponsors of liturgical reform in the United States, the Benedictines were fully cognizant of the move toward the centralized church. Among historical precedents to be considered for the new church was the small domed church of San Vitale, Ravenna (figs. 30,

31), suggested by Dom Aelred Graham, prior of the abbey school. Rejecting the traditional longitudinal plan in favor of a centralized one, the octagonal plan of San Vitale, where each of the eight sides might provide a private alcove for individual prayer, seemed especially apt.

Drawing on the traditional octagonal form, Belluschi used an exposed freestanding structural system of radiating laminated wood arches enclosed by non-loadbearing walls of wood and local fieldstone. Above the octagonal sanctuary is a second, smaller octagon, or dome, with stained-glass walls which cast brilliant colored light into the nave. Surmounting this is a still smaller octagonal cupola topped by a slender spire. On the interior, creating a dramatic focal point over the altar, is a filigree sculpture of thin, taut wire by the New York abstractionist Richard Lippold. The visual centerpiece of the whole, Lippold's gossamer network captures light from an inconspicuous skylight overhead, radiating it throughout the space of the sanctuary.

Well before the Portsmouth commission, Belluschi had promoted the integration of fine arts and architecture. The emotional power of architectural elements—space, light, color, texture—he felt was, or could be, enhanced by the use of stained glass, murals, sculpture, and other arts, especially in the church.[49] In the years before Belluschi moved to Cambridge, Portland was small and its pool of artistic talent

Fig. 32. Zen garden, Portsmouth Abbey,
ca. 1961 (1987 photograph).

limited. The East Coast, by contrast, with its generally more affluent, culturally sophisticated clients, and the resources of New York City, which in the 1950s was rapidly surpassing Paris as the artistic capital of the world, offered Belluschi's long-standing interest in the fine arts room to expand.

The Belluschi-Lippold collaboration at Portsmouth marked a new phase in Belluschi's work, and throughout the late 1950s and 1960s his buildings were often designed with a major artistic work in mind. He was not alone in this regard. Architects throughout the country were welcoming collaboration with contemporary artists as a way of regaining some of the humanism lost in the earlier phases of modernism.[50] Belluschi often acknowledged the importance of working with painters and sculptors whom he regarded, in Whiteheadian terms, "as participants in discovery." Together, he maintained, they could "find stimulus in the whole range of created things and the power to satisfy human emotions."[51]

Zen Buddhism was another interest of the Portsmouth fathers. In the late 1950s, while Belluschi was designing the abbey church, Dom Graham took a sabbatical to Japan to study the relationship between Zen and Western Christianity; this led to his book, *Zen Catholicism*, published in 1963. Regarding Zen as a form of meditation, a "pure experience" rather than a religious doctrine, Graham was interested in its essential spirituality transcending denominational differences.[52] He conceived of Zen as an answer to the modern search for certainty in an uncertain world, a philosophy of life universal in its application; Zen

meant having "a mind enlightened to the inevitable," bearing the calm of an inner harmony arising from the knowledge that the individual was part of nature.[53] Recognizing a breach between religion and daily life in Western religion, Graham saw Zen as a way of uniting the two in a continuum. As Belluschi was later to put it, Zen was considered "the essence of all religion, without being shackled by all the symbolism" and religious imagery of the Western church, a way of penetrating "to the core of one's spirit, to the unknowns of our existence." It was a quest for wisdom, "a search for a religion of our times."[54] One of the fathers at Portsmouth proposed a Zen garden on the north side of the church (fig. 32), which delighted Belluschi, already sympathetic to and experienced in Japanese architecture and landscaping.

The appeal of Zen lay in its emphasis on simplicity, discipline, and restraint. Of interest, too, was its sense of wonder or awe at the "givenness," the "ah-ness" of things, suggesting the poet's sensitivity to sight and sound, the beauty of common things, and awareness of their perishability—the Buddhist sense of the impermanence of all matter. Still another Zen concept was *yūgen*, the remote and mysterious, or that which cannot be easily grasped in words.[55] This Eastern sense of the ineffable and unknowable differed diametrically from the Western ideal of the clear and known. In architecture, the concept was the antithesis of the Miesian aesthetic, with its emphasis on Cartesian rationality and lucidity. These notions, running counter to the mainstream, affected not just the Portsmouth abbey but other churches Belluschi designed at this time.

Fig. 33. Temple Israel, Swampscott, Massachusetts, 1953–56 (1989 photograph).

Fig. 34. Temple Adath Israel, Merion, Pennsylvania, 1956–59 (1987 photograph).

Fig. 35. Temple B'rith Kodesh, Rochester, New York, 1959–63 (1987 photograph).

Belluschi's engagement with Japanese architecture dated at least to the late 1930s and his years in the Pacific Northwest. His first visit to Japan, however, did not take place until the summer of 1956, while he was working on the Portsmouth church. All the aspects of the Japanese tradition that had earlier struck a sympathetic chord—straightforwardness, use of wood, simple elegance and sense of refinement, economy of means, spatial progression, unobtrusiveness, and fit with the natural environment—again came to the fore.

By the mid-1950s, when Mies's influence was at its peak, the architectural profession at large shared this interest. A 1955 exhibition of Japanese architecture at the Museum of Modern Art in New York simultaneously reflected and stimulated the trend, paving the way for scores of publications on Japanese architecture and landscaping throughout the later 1950s and the 1960s. The basic characteristics of Japanese architecture—rational framed structure, modularity, open interiors, skilled craftsmanship—exhibited obvious parallels, for all the apparent differences, to the work of Mies. It was this same interest in a simple, economical architecture with its quiet repose, reticence, and harmony with nature, much of which Belluschi had gained through his exposure to Japanese architecture in the late 1930s, that accounted for the appeal of Belluschi's work in the late 1950s.

In 1953, shortly after receiving the Portsmouth commission, Belluschi was asked to design his first synagogue, Temple Israel in Swampscott, Massachusetts, just outside Boston (fig. 33, no. 14). The Jewish temple presented a new set of challenges. On the one hand, as

there was no commonly accepted architectural prototype, Belluschi was free from traditional design expectations; on the other hand, Jewish liturgical demands differed from those he was accustomed to. After immersing himself in the literature on Jewish customs, he conceived of the synagogue not so much as a house of God, as in the Christian tradition, but as a place for assembly, study, and prayer.[56] In short, the task was to design an explicit rationalized structure that made clear a transcendent purpose in distinctly Judaic terms.

Like the Portsmouth church, the sanctuary of the Swampscott synagogue is defined by an internally exposed, hexagonal framework of laminated wood and steel, enclosed by a six-sided dome glazed in pale stained glass. The interior, defined by a lightweight, peripheral structural system that functions like a tent, is thus entirely free of internal supports; as such, the building itself alludes to the Talmudic Tent of Meeting.

Several years later Belluschi explored the same concept of an explicit, lightweight, polygonal structure, in concrete rather than wood, at the Temple Adath Israel in Merion, Pennsylvania (fig. 34, no. 15), then in steel on a far larger scale at the Temple B'rith Kodesh in Rochester, New York (fig. 35, no. 20).

While he was working on the First Lutheran Church in Boston, the Portsmouth Abbey Church, and the Swampscott synagogue, Belluschi received a commission from yet another denomination. This one was to add a large sanctuary to the existing Church of the Redeemer for a conservative, well-to-do Episcopalian congregation in suburban

Fig. 36. Church of the Redeemer, Baltimore, Maryland, 1954–58 (1989 photograph).

Fig. 37. Church of the Redeemer. Interior.

Fig. 38. Saint-Serge, Angers, France, ca. 1215–20. Interior.

Baltimore (fig. 36, no. 17). Like the Cottage Grove Presbyterian, the church proved to be one of his finest works.

The demands were unusually difficult. The congregation wanted to keep the original small, stone 1858 English Parish church while adding a sanctuary that would more than quadruple its seating capacity; the new building was, however, to remain subordinate to the old, in both scale and effect. While remaining sympathetic to the old, the new church was to be communal rather than hierarchical in plan to meet new liturgical requirements. The biggest problem, however, which almost cost Belluschi the job, was the matter of style. His assumption that by coming to him the congregation sought a modern church proved unwarranted, and it was only after a prolonged battle that Belluschi and his associates, Rogers, Taliaferro and Lamb, won their case.

Collaborating closely with his associates, Belluschi arrived at a solution that combined the ideals of modernism—structural rationalism, honest and economical use of materials, nonhistoricizing, clean, simple, unornamented form—with the legacy of the traditional English Parish church. Maintaining the massing of the original, with roofs the same pitch and with projecting half-timbered gables, but altering the proportions of base to roof, the Belluschi team came up with a scheme that echoed the old church without replicating or overwhelming it, despite the difference in scale.

The high gabled roof dominates the form, borne on an internal framework of freestanding, exposed, laminated wood arches (fig. 37). Belluschi pursued here the same concept of a structural frame independent of a sheltering roof with non-loadbearing walls that he had initially explored in earlier churches, such as St. Thomas More and Zion Lutheran (nos. 3, 8); he would continue to explore the concept elsewhere, using different structural systems. Here, too, is Belluschi's familiar progression of spaces through a loggia into a small, private, landscaped courtyard, then into the darkened sanctuary. The focal point of the interior and climax of the spatial sequence is a brilliantly colored monumental glass window by the well-known artist Gyorgy Kepes, which fills the chancel wall behind the altar.

Though developed in an open collaboration with his associates, the design of the Church of the Redeemer remains unmistakably Belluschi's, governed by his concern for lucid structure, skillful dramatic lighting, progression of spaces, and a space mysterious and ambiguous yet lofty and inspirational. The church represents his ideals of church design at their clearest: a systematic structural rationality analogous to the Gothic (fig. 38) but fully modern, even Miesian, in its legibility; a space symbolic in its suggestion of both the finite and infinite; and dramatic light, subdued in the nave, brilliant over the altar—the whole surely the envy of an Abbot Suger.

Responding to the new liturgical demand for a communal space by means of a cross-axial plan, with the altar in the center, the Church of the Redeemer also answers the individual's need for a quiet, meditative space. Spare in its means yet resplendent in its effect, it responds to Tillich's appeal for a holy emptiness. Simple and serene, with a consistent visual order overseen by a single aesthetic sensibility—from site planning, architecture, landscaping, and art to details such as the color of the carpeting and the finish on the pews—it suggests the all-encompassing unity of Eastern thought. Particularly Zen is the sense of perishability: the etched cross, barely visible above the altar, evokes fleetingness and the impermanence of all things.

With its lucid structure and ineffable space, the building also speaks eloquently of Whitehead's idea of religion, "the vision of something which stands beyond, behind, and within, the passing flux of immediate things." The Church of the Redeemer is a *summa theologia*, embodying the ideas of some of the most important thinkers and theologians of the time. It marks a high point, not only in Belluschi's own work but in twentieth-century American church architecture.

By the end of the decade, Belluschi's skill as an architect of religious buildings was internationally recognized.[57] *Architectural Record* of 1959, remarking on his exceptional gift, made a telling point: his success was due not to a "knack" or his "fine Italian hand" but rather to his profound understanding of the issues involved. Underlying his controlled geometries, his beautifully ordered churches, was a deeper understanding:

> One finds an aesthetic of humility, simplicity and discipline. A warm feeling for the people of the congregation strengthens his ability to give form to their aspiration. There is no hint of subjective isolation, or unrelated self-expression; Belluschi's discipline and objectivity are complete, his involvement absolute.

The author pointed out that Belluschi was known primarily for his earlier churches in the Pacific Northwest. His new work in the East, however, differing widely in circumstances and in faiths—Catholic, Lutheran, Jewish, Episcopalian—offered "further evidence of the power of Belluschi's talent, backed by the vigor of his conviction."[58]

The 1960s

In December 1960, Mies van der Rohe was quoted in a *Time Magazine* article on new modern churches as saying: "This is not a great cathedral-building age. Today, if you tried to build a cathedral, you would succeed only in building a big church. Not religion but technology is the controlling spirit of the age." Interviewed for the same article, Belluschi reluctantly agreed but, in light of society's persistent spiritual need, saw the situation as a challenge: "If we cannot erect great monuments, we may endeavor to create small temples on a more human scale, designed in a sensitive manner so as to produce the kind of atmosphere most conducive to worship."[59]

The article was illustrated by Frank Lloyd Wright's project for a Congregational church in Redding, California (fig. 39). It also discussed Marcel Breuer's new church at St. John's Abbey in Minnesota (see fig. 23) with its 112-foot-high parabolic bell banner of reinforced concrete that the architect maintained was "as expressive of the mid-20th century as the Byzantine, Roman and Gothic arch and spire were of theirs." Presenting a different approach, Belluschi again cautioned readers of the dangers of structural exhibitionism: "A simple church is always better than an elaborate one. Church design should be an exercise in restraint, in understatement."

Simplicity became the theme of one of Belluschi's most important addresses, delivered at a national conference on church architecture in Seattle in March 1963 and published in *Architectural Record* several months later ("Eloquent Simplicity in Architecture," Appendix). After a decade of celebrating the artist-architect, and the appearance of new, often startling sculptural forms by one star architect after another, Belluschi was asked to make a case "for those simple qualities which are the basis of all enduring architecture."

Characteristically he zeroed in on the heart of the matter. The church belonged to the congregation, not to the architect. It was *their* vision, *their* spiritual aspirations he was asked to express. The church architect, he said, had to be humble in the sense of "being of the earth, of partaking of the eternal balance of nature." He had to forgo the formalistic or stylistic concerns of his profession, resist the lure of making a personal artistic statement, and be willing instead "to open his heart

Fig. 39. Frank Lloyd Wright, Pilgrim Congregational Church (project), Redding, California, 1958.

Fig. 40. Louis Kahn, Unitarian Church, Rochester, New York, 1959–67.

Fig. 41. I. M. Pei, National Center for Atmospheric Research, Boulder, Colorado, 1961–67.

as well as his mind to the faith which animates the religious world." It was this, Belluschi's ability truly to listen, that kept him in touch with the spiritual values of the age, enabling him to discern those symbols that still carried meaning, and to distinguish timeless values from the merely ephemeral.

Belluschi spoke of the simple qualities at the base of all enduring architecture. This was not the simplicity of the fool, but that of the saint, and "the result of deep understanding and purification, of an act which has gone through the fires of passion and reason." By means of this simplicity the architect was able to grasp the essence of the church and express its purpose.

Drawing on Tillich, Belluschi maintained the church was more than mere shelter. Its finite space implied the infinite of which it was only a part, providing protection but also conveying a more profound purpose. Belluschi drew, too, on Whitehead and the permanence of change. Human affairs were never stagnant, and architecture had always been compelled to come to terms with change. Creative individuals were forever probing beyond the known, refusing to be awed by the past and be content merely to imitate; to do so denied the spiritual values of the time and their own creative gifts. Beauty would emerge, Belluschi said, by simple adherence to St. Thomas Aquinas's three

principles of art—integrity, proportion, and clarity—rather than through new tricks of the trade. Innovation should be motivated by an inner longing, a vision or insight that demanded expression rather than the desire to exploit a new structural system for its own sake. For the architect, this called for discipline, avoiding the seduction of new forms and techniques, discriminating, paring down, and refining his work until it "sings with purpose and unity."

The decade of the 1960s was tumultuous, architecturally as well as socially and politically. Sympathies shifted from Miesian structuralism to Corbusian plasticity; tastes changed from the delicately textured, screened, explicit, lightweight structures of the 1950s to the hefty, muscular, more massive, Kahn- and Corbusier-inspired Brutalist forms of the 1960s (fig. 40). Belluschi was one of the midwives of the new trend: he was instrumental in selecting I. M. Pei as architect for the National Center for Atmospheric Research in Boulder, Colorado, a complex, asymmetrical, highly plastic composition of bold, solid, geometric forms in concrete (fig. 41), and was spokesman for the jurors of the Boston City Hall competition who selected Kallmann, McKinnell and Knowles's robust, monumental sculptural proposal.[60]

By the 1960s Belluschi was working out of the Cambridge office of the young Argentinian architect Eduardo Catalano, whom he had

Fig. 42. Church of the Christian Union, Rockford, Illinois, 1962–66.

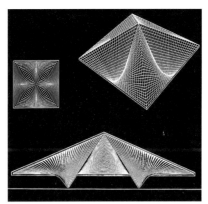

Fig. 43. Eduardo Catalano. *Structures of Warped Surfaces*. The Student Publication of the School of Design, vol. 10, no. 1 (Raleigh, N.C., 1960).

Fig. 44. Kenzo Tange, St. Mary's Cathedral, Tokyo, 1961–64.

brought to MIT as a professor of architecture. Catalano's work in shell technology and structures of warped surfaces, much of it inspired by the late sculptural buildings of Le Corbusier, was of great interest to Belluschi. Keenly aware of changing values and mindful, too, of Tillich's concept of the church building as a symbol, Belluschi moved away from his smaller, reticent, wooden buildings toward larger, bold, sculptural forms of concrete. The series of churches in the Midwest of the early 1960s—the First Community Church project in Columbus, Ohio (no. 23), the First Methodist Church in Duluth, Minnesota (no. 24), and the Church of the Christian Union in Rockford, Illinois (fig. 42, no. 25)—all pursued this more vigorous, sculptural vein.

The 1963 commission for St. Mary's Cathedral in San Francisco offered Belluschi the chance of a lifetime: to design and build a twentieth-century cathedral, fully expressive of the modern era, in one of the most earthquake-prone, architecturally self-conscious cities in the world (no. 26). It also faced Belluschi squarely against the Miesian challenge. Inspired by Catalano's work in warped surfaces (fig. 43) as well as Tange's St. Mary's Cathedral in Tokyo (fig. 44), Belluschi envisioned the new cathedral as a monumental sculpture composed of eight sweeping concrete hyperbolic paraboloids rising from a square plan to form a single cross-shaped vault, with all the forces of the soaring vault

funneled down onto four massive concrete pylons in each corner (fig. 45). Experimenting with progressive structural technology—indeed, pushing its very limits, Belluschi conceived of St. Mary's as a memorable symbolic image, a bold, sculptural form large enough to exert a monumental presence yet not overwhelm the delicate nineteenth-century scale of the city. Even here, however, Belluschi's main goal was to create a compelling spiritual space equal to any in the world.

He visualized the new cathedral as an all-encompassing work of art like Notre Dame in Paris or St. Peter's in Rome, with architecture, painting, sculpture, stained glass, furnishings, even music, united in a single artistic entity. The building itself was further to be linked visually to the city as a whole, integrated into daily life as one aesthetic continuum, symbolizing the unity of the spiritual and secular.

In designing St. Mary's, Belluschi had faced enormous odds. The Bay Area during the early 1960s was one of the nation's hotbeds of social and political unrest. In 1964, one year after the cathedral was commissioned, the Free Speech movement erupted on the Berkeley campus of the University of California. Four years later, as pressure mounted and tempers flared, San Francisco became the focus of a series of antidevelopment protests, a backlash against the rise of corporate towers, monumental elitist cultural centers, and large-scale urban

Fig. 45. St. Mary's Cathedral, San Francisco, 1963–70.

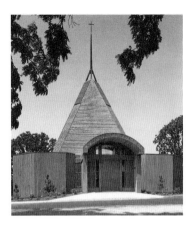

Fig. 46. Immanuel Lutheran Church, Silverton, Oregon, 1975–79.

Fig. 47. University of Portland Chapel, Portland, Oregon, 1985–86 (1987 photograph).

redevelopment projects being built, protesters maintained, at the expense of low-cost housing. St. Mary's was seized as a conspicuous example of the expenditure of millions of dollars many felt should go to the poor, and became symbolic of the nation's discontent. Months of struggling with Pier Luigi Nervi to work out a feasible structural system, long negotiations with city engineers who questioned the structure's safety, debates with the design review board of the Redevelopment Agency, on whose land the cathedral was built, and lengthy discussions with the archbishop over the radicalism of abstract art all took their toll on Belluschi's energy. As rounds of public protest continued to delay construction and inflation set in, by the late 1960s his spirits sagged. Architecture was no longer the creative search Whitehead had spoken of, an artistic adventure exploring the unknown, but a matter of process. It drained the profession of much of its glamour.

As his experimentation with hyperbolic paraboloids and thin-shell structure in St. Mary's progressed, Belluschi continued to work in the more muscular, Brutalist direction being pursued by architects such as Kahn, Saarinen, and Rudolph. St. Margaret of Cortona (no. 27) was designed at this time. Its thick blank walls, rough textured surfaces, bold asymmetrical forms, and irregular roofline all bear evidence of architects' growing interest in vernacular architecture.

In the late 1960s, as the influence of established churches waned, and demand for new church buildings dropped, Belluschi

turned to a quieter, simpler, less obtrusive formal language. Constructed in these same years were the Bishop W. Angie Smith Chapel in Oklahoma City (no. 30) and the Fort Myer Post Chapel in Norfolk, Virginia (no. 35), with a simple geometric form defined by a folded-slab roof hovering like a tent or poised canopy over a centralized sanctuary.

The 1970s and 1980s

Belluschi retired from the deanship at MIT in 1965 but remained in Boston as a design consultant, working mostly on high-rise office buildings and other commercial or institutional projects. In 1973, after receiving the American Institute of Architects gold medal, the organization's highest award, Belluschi moved back to Portland. One of his first commissions on his return was the Immanuel Lutheran Church in Silverton, a small rural community south of Portland, whose original Gothic Revival building he had enlarged in 1947 (no. 7) and again in 1966 (no. 32). In 1975 the church was destroyed by fire, and Belluschi was asked back to design a wholly new building. The new church (fig. 46, no. 36), a simple polyhedron resting on a broad base and terminating in a tall slender steeple, was the first of a series of late churches around Portland in which Belluschi continued his earlier regional approach of small, unpretentious buildings, mostly of brick or wood.

Fig. 48. Old Ship Meeting House, Hingham, Massachusetts, 1681–1755.

Fig. 49. Brookman Whitehouse, Temple Beth-Israel, Portland, Oregon, 1927 (1991 photograph).

Fig. 50. United Hebrew Synagogue (under construction), St. Louis, Missouri, 1986–89.

These were characterized by their domestic scale, dominant rooflines, and interiors of exposed framed structure and unpainted wood.

Attitudes toward the church had by this time once again changed. After a pause in the late 1960s when a virtual moratorium was placed on monumental church building, a revival of religious values in the 1970s led many members of the church community to return to a pre-Constantinian concept of the church, or the "non-church," where people gathered in homes. The church building was seen simply as a functional meeting place, a secular house of people rather than a sacred house of God.[61] Belluschi's small, domestically scaled structures, such as the University of Portland Chapel (fig. 47, no. 38), though still distinctly a "church," reflected this thinking.

Intended to serve as a student center as well as a church, and to be modern yet fit the predominantly Georgian campus, the University of Portland Chapel is a quiet, understated building of brick and wood. The chapel has a sweeping gabled, hipped roof and welcoming portico; a simple glazed cupola marks the centralized auditorium space. Influenced formally by Belluschi's simple regional churches of the 1940s, the building, in its joint secular and spiritual functions, also harks back, if only symbolically, to the plain, four-square, hipped roof of the New England meetinghouse and its identifying cupola and spire (fig. 48).

Very different in both problem and solution was the late 1980s commission for a large Jewish synagogue in St. Louis. Abstracting a traditional type provided by a revivalist, Byzantine-inspired synagogue of 1927 in Portland (fig. 49), Belluschi created a domed, monumental building that drew on tradition but was unmistakably modern in form (fig. 50, no. 40).

In 1979, after over half a century of designing sacred buildings throughout the country for a broad range of faiths, Belluschi was asked to deliver a speech in Phoenix on religious architecture, an appropriate role for one with a wealth of experience rare among architects and the insight that comes only with deep thought.

The design of a house of worship was to Belluschi more than merely meeting practical demands. It was more than skillful handling of the architectural language, using structurally convincing volumes, subtly manipulating light and shadow, creating a temporal progression of spaces, or arriving at an appropriate sense of scale. To him, it meant understanding the fundamental role of the religious institution in contemporary society, interpreting the spiritual values of those for whom he built, and ultimately coming to terms with his own relationship with God ("Architects and Artists: Interpreting Man's Spiritual Dreams," Appendix).

Belluschi's churches are more than architectural experiments, more, too, than simply a moving aesthetic experience. His controlled geometries and lucid structures suggest the power of reason, the presence of a comprehensible system; his darkened, ambiguous spaces evoke a sense of mystery, arousing but not fully satisfying, in Whiteheadian terms, one's search for basic answers. What mattered to Belluschi was not just architecture's external form but the full experience of its presence and space. He sought a reticent exterior that bespoke both a symbolic function as a communal place of worship, and a quiet meditative interior with a profoundly sacred space. His religious buildings stand as a personal interpretation of mankind's spiritual dreams, embodying his broad and deep understanding of the relationship between the individual and God, the known and the unknown, and the sense of one's finiteness in the larger universal realm.

NOTES

1. Interview transcript, "Tape-recorded Interview with Pietro Belluschi in Portland, Oregon. August 22–23, September 4, 1983. Meredith L. Clausen, interviewer." Archives of American Art, Smithsonian Institution, Washington, D.C., 1983. Northwest Oral History Project, Pietro Belluschi, NWOHP, No. 12, pp. 2–3. All tapes except for those recorded for the Smithsonian Institution are in my possession and will remain so until the completion of the Belluschi monograph. They will then be donated to either the Oregon Historical Society, Portland, or the George Arents Research Library, Syracuse University, Syracuse, New York.

There is as yet no major publication on Belluschi's entire life and career, a gap my monograph, *Pietro Belluschi: Modern American Architect*, to be published by MIT Press, attempts to fill. *The Northwest Architecture of Pietro Belluschi* (ed. Jo Stubblebine [New York: F. W. Dodge, 1953]) consists mainly of photographs of his early Oregon work and excerpts from his speeches; it covers only the first half of his career. *Pietro Belluschi: Edifici e progetti, 1932–73*, exh. cat. (Rome: Officina Edizioni, 1974), by Camillo Gubitosi and Alberto Izzo, is a good but highly selective catalogue of some of his major buildings.

For a more comprehensive description of his life and career, I recommend one of the entries in a standard encyclopedia, or my own essay in the *Encyclopedia of Architecture, Design, Engineering, and Construction*, ed. Joseph A. Wilkes and Robert T. Packard (New York: John Wiley & Sons, 1988), vol. 1, pp. 443–48.

2. For a fuller discussion of the Doyle office and Belluschi's professional practice in the Portland years, as well as an analysis of one of his most celebrated commercial buildings, see my article "Belluschi and the Equitable Building in History," *Journal of the Society of Architectural Historians* 50, no. 2 (June 1991): 109–29; and *Pietro Belluschi: Modern American Architect*, forthcoming.

3. *Pacific Builder and Engineer* 44 (Oct. 15, 1938): 3.

4. Belluschi, "Report on Project for Catholic Church Submitted by the Catholic Diocese of Portland," unpublished, 1936 (Belluschi Collection, George Arents Research Library, Syracuse University).

5. Clausen, "Belluschi and the Equitable Building in History," pp. 122–25, and *Pietro Belluschi: Modern American Architect*.

6. Frank Lloyd Wright, *Modern Architecture: Being the Kahn Lectures for 1930*, Princeton Monographs in Art and Archeology (Princeton, N.J.: Princeton University Press, 1931). On the Kahn lectures, see also Frederick Gutheim, "The Turning Point in Mr. Wright's Career," *American Institute of Architects Journal* 69, no. 4 (June 1980): 48. Belluschi's letter to Wright, dated July 2, 1931, is in the Belluschi private collection. Wright's response to Belluschi is published in B. B. Pfeiffer, ed., *Frank Lloyd Wright, Letters to Architects* (Fresno, Calif.: The Press at California State University, 1984), pp. 88–89.

7. It might be noted that in an interview in January 1991, Belluschi could say little of the Arts and Crafts movement, or of Wentz's interest in it. When asked about the Prairie School architect William Gray Purcell who had moved to Portland in 1920, Belluschi said only that he personally never liked Purcell, though he remembered his lectures on Sullivan's midwestern banks. The names of William C. Elmslie, Charles F. A. Voysey, and C. R. Ashbee meant nothing to him; taped interview, Belluschi with author, Jan. 19, 1991.

Bernard Maybeck's work, and that of Greene and Greene, Belluschi of course knew well. A copy of *The Life-Work of the American Architect Frank Lloyd Wright*, ed. H. Th. Wijdeveld (Santpoort, Holland: C. A. Mees, 1925), was in the Doyle library and is now in Belluschi's possession. When and by whom it was purchased, however, is unclear.

8. Charles Keeler, *The Simple Home* (San Francisco: Paul Elder & Co., 1904; Santa Barbara and Salt Lake City: Peregrine Smith, 1979), pp. 36–38. *The Simple Home* was the bible of the Hillside Club, the community of artists and architects in the Bay Area of which Maybeck was a part.

On the American Arts and Crafts movement, see Leslie Greene Bowman, *American Arts and Crafts: Virtue in Design*, exh. cat. (Los Angeles County Museum of Art, 1990), and Robert Judson Clark, ed., *The Arts and Crafts Movement in America, 1876–1916*, exh. cat. (Princeton, N.J.: Princeton University Press, 1972).

I thank my brother, Jack L. Clausen, who, knowing of my interests, brought *The Simple Home* to my attention.

9. The Wentz project also served as a prototype for a model home in the Pacific Northwest Home Show in Portland in 1938. On this connection, see Clausen, *Pietro Belluschi: Modern American Architect.*

10. Antonin Raymond, *Architectural Details* (1937; New York: Architectural Book Publishing Co., 1947). Letter ordering a copy, dated Mar. 15, 1939, in Belluschi Collection, George Arents Research Library, Syracuse University. The book was also the source of much of the detailing in Belluschi's domestic work, such as the Joss House near the St. Thomas More church in Portland of the same time.

11. An interest in the arts of Japan was widespread in the Portland community at this time. Wentz himself had an important collection of Japanese prints, which he later donated to the Portland Art Museum. Jiro Harada, the author of *The Lesson of Japanese Architecture*, first published in 1936 (rev. ed. [London: The Studio Ltd., 1954]), had lectured at the Portland Art Museum in December 1936 and again in early 1937. As an active member of the Portland Art Association as well as the architect of the museum building, then undergoing the addition of its second wing, Belluschi surely knew of these lectures.

Bruno Taut's much discussed *Houses and People of Japan* (London: John Gifford Ltd., 1937) quite likely further stimulated Belluschi's interest in Japanese architecture, as he was at this point growing increasingly aware of the importance of architectural trends beyond the purely local.

Two other formative influences should be mentioned in this context: John Yeon, whose Watzek House, which he designed while working in the Doyle office, contributed greatly to Belluschi's awareness of the possibilities of wood, and Paul Thiry, another major church designer in the Pacific Northwest who had visited Japan in 1933 and made the acquaintance of Antonin Raymond at that time. On Thiry and the influence of Japanese architecture in his work, see Meredith L. Clausen, "Paul Thiry and the Emergence of Modernism in the Pacific Northwest," *Pacific Northwest Quarterly* 75 (July 1984): 128–39.

12. Walter Gordon, "Designed by Pietro Belluschi," *Pencil Points* 23, no. 7 (July 1942): 59–63, 75. Gordon was one of the architects in the Belluschi office.

13. On Belluschi's work during World War II and his assumption of the Doyle office, see Clausen, *Pietro Belluschi: Modern American Architect.*

14. Clausen, "Paul Thiry and the Emergence of Modernism."

15. Henry May, "Religion and American Intellectual History, 1945–1985: Reflections on an Uneasy Relationship," in *Religion and Twentieth-Century American Intellectual Life*, ed. Michael J. Lacey (Cambridge, England: Woodrow Wilson International Center for Scholars and Cambridge University Press, 1989), pp. 12–22; Robert Wuthnow, *The Restructuring of American Religion, Society and Faith since World War II* (Princeton, N.J.: Princeton University Press, 1988), pp. 14–53.

16. F. S. C. Northrop, *The Meeting of East and West: An Inquiry Concerning World Understanding* (New York: The Macmillan Company, 1946), esp. chaps. 9 and 10.

17. James Alfred Martin, Jr., "Holiness and Beauty in Eastern Thought," in *Beauty and Holiness: The Dialogue between Aesthetics and Religion* (Princeton, N.J.: Princeton University Press, 1990), pp. 136–63; Northrop, *Meeting of East and West*, pp. 312–22.

18. Taped interview, Belluschi with author, Oct. 13, 1990.

19. Wuthnow, *Restructuring of American Religion*, p. 15.

20. William Ward Watkin, *Planning and Building the Modern Church* (New York: F. W. Dodge, 1951), p. 6.

21. Letter, Belluschi to Lawrence B. Anderson, Aug. 24, 1984, Belluschi personal collection; taped interview, Belluschi with author, Mar. 2, 1990. Anderson was a professor of architecture at MIT while Belluschi was dean and succeeded him as dean; the two worked as associates on several projects, including the Portsmouth Abbey church (no. 13).

22. According to Belluschi, he has had the Newsom book "for as long as I can remember," and it remains one of his fondest possessions. Taped interview, Belluschi with author, Dec. 9, 1986. See also Clausen, *Pietro Belluschi: Modern*

American Architect, on the Japanese influence in the Pacific Northwest.

23. Taped interview, D. Hugh Peniston with author, May 19, 1990. Peniston was the pastor of the Cottage Grove Presbyterian at the time it was built.

24. "The Architect and His Community: Pietro Belluschi," *Progressive Architecture* 30, no. 2 (Feb. 1949): 40–41. See also Clausen, *Pietro Belluschi: Modern American Architect*, in which I discuss in detail Belluschi's practice before and after his move east.

25. Peter Hammond, *Liturgy and Architecture* (London: William Clowes & Sons, Ltd., 1960), esp. chaps. 2, 4, and 6, and *Church Architecture: The Shape of Reform* (Washington, D.C.: The Liturgical Conference, 1965).

26. "Building Types Study No. 272: Pietro Belluschi," *Architectural Record* 126, no. 1 (July 1959): 154.

27. Louis Cassels, "New Age of Faith Sparks Church Boom," *Nation's Business* 44, no. 2 (Feb. 1956): 92.

28. Taped interview, Belluschi with author, Dec. 17, 1986.

29. "Architecture To-Day: A Symposium," Appendix.

30. Taped interviews: Bill Weber of Skidmore, Owings & Merrill with author, San Francisco, June 24, 1986; Lawrence B. Anderson with author, Sept. 16, 1987. See also Belluschi, "The Meaning of Regionalism in Architecture," *Architectural Record* 118, no. 6 (Dec. 1955): 132.

31. Letter, Belluschi to author, Feb. 24, 1986; taped interviews, Belluschi with author, Apr. 14, 1990, and Oct. 13, 1990.

32. Charles Hartshorne and Creighton Peden, *Whitehead's View of Reality* (New York: Pilgrim Press, 1981), p. 85; taped interview, Belluschi with author, Apr. 14, 1990.

33. Lucien Price, "To Live without Certitude: Dialogues of Whitehead," *Atlantic Monthly* 193, no. 3 (Mar. 1954): 57–61; "The Permanence of Change: Dialogues of Whitehead," *Atlantic Monthly* 193, no. 4 (Apr. 1954): 67–71 (copy in Belluschi's personal collection); Lucien Price, *Dialogues of Alfred North Whitehead* (Boston: Little, Brown and Company, 1954) (heavily underlined copy in Belluschi's library).

34. Pietro Belluschi, "A New Century of Architecture," *American Institute of Architects Journal* 28, no. 2 (June 1957): 182.

35. Taped interviews, Belluschi with author, for example, Oct. 13, 1990.

36. Hartshorne and Peden, *Whitehead's View of Reality*, pp. 7, 22, 35; Martin, *Beauty and Holiness*, pp. 120–23. As is often noted, Whitehead's writing tends to be obscure, leaving his work open to a number of different interpretations. See A. H. Johnson, *Whitehead's Theory of Reality* (Boston: Beacon Press, 1952), p. xii, and more recently, A. W. Masters, "Epitaph for a Metaphysician," review of Victor Lowe, *Alfred North Whitehead: The Man and His Work*, vols. 1 and 2, in *Times Literary Supplement*, Dec. 7–13, 1990, 1329.

37. Paul Tillich, "Theology and Architecture," *Architectural Forum* 103, no. 6 (Dec. 1955): 130–37.

38. Paul Tillich, "Religion as a Dimension in Man's Spiritual Life," in *Theology of Culture*, ed. Robert C. Kimball (New York: Oxford University Press, 1959), pp. 3–9.

39. Paul Tillich, *On Art and Architecture*, ed. John Dillenberger and Jane Dillenberger (New York: Crossroad Publishing Co., 1987), introduction, and Tillich, "Systematic Theology" [1963], pp. 160–61. See also Tillich's "The Nature of Religious Language," in ibid., pp. 53–67.

40. Tillich, "Theology and Architecture," 133; Tillich, "Existentialist Aspects of Modern Art" [1956], in *On Art and Architecture*, p. 95 and passim.

41. Tillich, "Visual Arts and the Revelatory Character of Style," lecture delivered at Columbia University, 1958, in *On Art and Architecture*, pp. 126–38; Tillich, "Theology and Architecture," 134.

42. Tillich, "On the Theology of Fine Arts and Architecture," in *On Art and Architecture*, pp. 211–12. See also his "Nature of Religious Language," in *Theology of Culture*, p. 54.

43. Paul Tillich, "Environment and the Individual," address delivered at the AIA national convention, Washington, D.C., May 14, 1957, published in *American Institute of Architects Journal* 28, no. 2 (June 1957): 90–92.

44. Tillich, "Honesty and Consecration in Art and Architecture," lecture delivered at the twenty-sixth National Conference on Church Architecture, Chicago, Apr. 1965, in *On Art and Architecture*, p. 226.

45. Tillich, "Theology and Architecture," 193.

46. Ibid., 192, and Tillich, "Honesty and Consecration," p. 227; Belluschi, "Eloquent Simplicity in Church Design," and "Architects and Artists: Interpreting Man's Spiritual Dreams," Appendix.

47. Letter, D. Hugh Peniston to Belluschi, Nov. 20, 1979, Belluschi personal collection; taped interview, Hugh Peniston with author, May 19, 1990.

48. Taped interview, Rev. Dom Peter Sidler, Portsmouth Abbey,

with author, Apr. 1, 1989.

49. See, for example, his remarks in "Architecture To-Day: A Symposium," Appendix.

50. Eleanor Bittermann, *Art in Modern Architecture* (New York: Reinhold Publishing, 1952), pp. 3–4. For a discussion of the relationship of art and architecture in the religious setting specifically mentioning Belluschi, see also John Dillenberger, "Art and Architecture in the Religious Community," *Faith and Form. Journal of the Guild for Religious Architecture/Affiliate of the American Institute of Architects* 13 (Fall 1980): 30. Dillenberger and his wife, Jane, were the editors of *On Art and Architecture*.

51. Belluschi, "The Challenge of St. John's Cathedral," Appendix.

52. Dom Aelred Graham, *Zen Catholicism: A Suggestion* (New York: Harcourt Brace & World, 1963), p. 29.

53. Ibid., pp. xiii, 25–34, 155.

54. Taped interview, Belluschi with author, Apr. 14, 1990. See also Graham, *Zen Catholicism*, p. 141.

55. Martin, *Beauty and Holiness*, p. 162.

56. Belluschi, "Notes on the Design of Temple Adath Israel, Merion, Pa., 1 April 1957" (unpublished manuscript, George Arents Research Library, Syracuse University). See also Harold W. Turner, *From Temple to Meeting House: The Phenomenology and Theology of Places of Worship* (The Hague: Mouton Publishers, 1979), chap. 6, where the author distinguishes between temple and synagogue, a distinction Belluschi does not make.

57. See, for example, Roberto Aloi, *Architettura funerio moderna* (Milan: U. Hoepli, 1948), pp. 98–100; *World's Contemporary Architecture*, ed. Ino Yuichi (Tokyo: Shokokusha Publishing, 1953), vol. 2, pp. 38–39, and vol. 6, pp. 50–51; and Willy Weyres and Otto Bartning, *Kirchen Handbuch für den Kirchenbau* (Munich: Verlag Georg D. W. Callwey, 1958), pp. 344–45.

58. "Building Types Study No. 272," p. 147.

59. "The New Churches," *Time Magazine*, Dec. 26, 1960, 28.

60. For more on Belluschi's role as architectural adviser and juror, a role in which he wielded tremendous power especially in the 1960s, see Clausen, *Pietro Belluschi: Modern American Architect*.

61. Edward A. Sövik, *Architecture for Worship* (Minneapolis: Augsburg Publishing House, 1973), p. 39.

EARLY CHURCHES, PACIFIC NORTHWEST

MORNINGLIGHT CHAPEL, FINLEY MORTUARY

New chapel for the Finley Mortuary, Portland, Oregon (1936–37; demolished 1985)
Architect: A. E. Doyle & Associates; designer: Pietro Belluschi
Cost excluding architect's fee: $105,000

The Finley Mortuary, founded in 1892, was Oregon's oldest mortuary establishment. Housed in a large, stately, stuccoed building, a 1912 Colonial Revival structure, the mortuary by 1936 needed more room. The added portion was to include a new, distinctly modern chapel that clearly and simply stated its functional purpose. Though nondenominational, it was to be spiritual in character. As the chapel was sited on the corner of a busy city street, visual privacy and noise insulation were essential. The building was to exert presence yet avoid pretension and convey a sense of quiet dignity.

The project consisted of three components: remodeling the existing building to bring it up-to-date with the new portions; adding a middle unit containing reception and administration quarters that would serve as a circulation center for the entire complex; and constructing a large chapel, with private facilities for small family gatherings, the minister, and pallbearers, and a sanctuary for memorial services with seating for 250.

Drawing on recent trends in modern architecture abroad, especially Scandinavian and Dutch examples published in such books as F. R. Yerbury's *Modern Dutch Buildings* (London: Ernest Benn, 1931), to which Belluschi had access in the Doyle office library, the Morninglight Chapel was thoroughly modern in its simple, bold, geometric forms, slender colonnaded loggia, and plain, powerful rectangular tower block. Of reinforced concrete, it had exteriors of warm red brick in a richly textured Flemish bond and limestone trim. Over the entrance

PLAN

EXISTING BLDG.

FEET 0 35

was a stylized bas-relief of a winged angel flanked by the Greek letters alpha and omega, evidently inspired by a small brick crematorium chapel in Copenhagen, a photograph of which Belluschi had pinned above his drafting table.

The chapel was parabolic in plan, with a longitudinal axis providing a focal point for the casket in the apse. The pulpit was to one side. Forming the back wall of the apse was a series of folding screens perforated in a repeated, stylized geometric pattern, relating to the decorative tiles used on the exterior at the base of the tower; these screens opened onto a waiting room for the family behind the apse.

The interior consisted of a simple high space covered by a flat ceiling of acoustical tiling. Abundant light came from a continuous clerestory of glass brick at the top of the high nave wall; the apse itself was lit by a large oculus. The walls were a soft ivory to reflect light, with side aisles and lobby paneled in dark Philippine mahogany. Belluschi's aim was to create a quiet, cleanly defined space, well lit but without glare.

The Finley chapel drew national attention for both its modernity and its carefully reasoned solution to a difficult circulation problem requiring the complete separation of, but smooth and efficient communication between, public and administrative spaces. It was selected by the American Institute of Architects as one of the one hundred outstanding buildings built in the United States since World War I, was awarded an honorable mention by the Architectural League of New York in 1937, and received a national American Institute of Architects award of merit the following year.

REFERENCES

"New Portland Mortuary to Be Built." *Oregonian Daily Newspaper* [Portland], Aug. 2, 1936.

Mortuary Management (Sept. 1937): 11–16.

"Mortuary for J. P. Finley and Son, Portland, Oregon." *Architectural Forum* 67, no. 6 (Dec. 1937): 468–70.

"Portland Mortuary Design Wins A.I.A. Award of Merit." *Pacific Builder and Engineer* 44 (Oct. 15, 1938): 3–4.

Aloi, Roberto. *Architettura funerio moderna* (Milan: U. Hoepli, 1948).

"The Northwest Architecture of Pietro Belluschi." *Architectural Record* 113, no. 4 (Apr. 1953): 137.

Taped interviews, Frank Allen with author, Dec. 6, 1986, and May 29, 1987 (Allen was an architect in the Doyle, then Belluschi, office in the 1930s and 1940s); George C. Finley with author, Jan. 18, 1991 (Finley is currently the vice president of the Finley Mortuary).

2. RIVERVIEW CEMETERY CHAPEL

Small memorial chapel for the Riverview Cemetery, Portland, Oregon (1939–40)
Architect: A. E. Doyle & Associates; designer: Pietro Belluschi
Cost: $73,848

The Riverview Chapel was part of a complex of buildings for the Riverview Cemetery, which was founded in the 1880s in the thickly wooded hills overlooking the city of Portland above the Willamette River. Belluschi's work included the design of a crematorium, offices, mausoleum, and columbarium as well as a new chapel. Tudor in character to harmonize with the landscaped, rural setting, the chapel was greatly simplified and distinctly modern in keeping with both progressive tastes and the straitened economy. Its crisp, unarticulated brick forms, banks of tall, narrow, rectangular, mullioned windows, and landscaped trellises bear evidence of the influence of both Louis Sullivan and Frank Lloyd Wright. The roofline also suggests a Japanese rather than Tudor influence, despite the building's otherwise traditional character.

The reinforced concrete structure is veneered in a deep reddish, richly textured brick. The chapel originally had white plastered walls and was vaulted by a system of exposed concrete arches. The bank of mullioned windows along the east side brought a low, even light into the nave; a rose window in the apse provided the principal source of light. Other public spaces such as the lobby, corridors, and vaults were veneered in marble.

The interiors have since been modified.

3. ST. THOMAS MORE CATHOLIC CHURCH

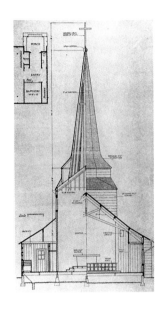

Small Catholic church in Portland, Oregon (1939–40)
Architect: A. E. Doyle & Associates; designer: Pietro Belluschi
Cost: $12,500

The Catholic parish of St. Thomas More had been using a small wood-frame Gothic Revival church, originally destined for Congregationalists, in the hills on the western edge of Portland. As the neighborhood and thus the parish's membership grew in the late 1930s, the old church proved too small. In the fall of 1939, Belluschi was commissioned to design a new church.

He faced a very tight budget which ultimately worked in his favor by forcing him to make the most of what was at hand. The site was at the crest of a hill just above a major intersection in a still largely rural but rapidly growing area on the west side of Portland. Ultimately inspired by the Wentz cottage (see figs. 4, 5), but drawing too on the work of Frank Lloyd Wright, the American Arts and Crafts movement, and the current work of Antonin Raymond and Japanese carpentry, Belluschi designed a distinctly modern church entirely of local materials.

St. Thomas More consists of a one-and-a-half-story rectangular building basically domestic in form, with a double-sloped pitched roof and shallow, extended eaves. A tall wooden steeple rising from an octagonal base set on a glazed square lantern marks the chancel at the far end. The slope of the site argued against a traditional axial entrance; instead, one enters through a simple, wooden porch at right angles to the nave, then pivots in the narthex to enter the sanctuary. The altar is at the far end of the long nave, with the choir and the sacristy to either side.

The unfinished knotty pine exteriors have been stained with a protective coating of lead and oil and allowed to weather naturally. The

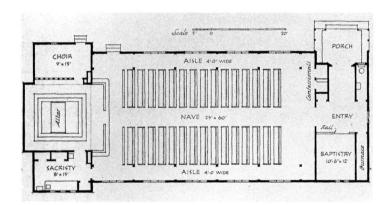

tal, symbolizing the gate to heaven, was defined simply and honestly with a richly grained cedar handcrafted in a lozenge pattern, its beauty derived solely from the inherent properties of the material.

Simple, humble, unpretentious in character, built with the utmost economy of means, St. Thomas More was Belluschi's first wooden church. Breaking from the prevailing traditions of the Gothic Revival type and the New England Colonial church with monumental pediment and cupola, it was published nationally in recognition of its modernity.

In 1948 the Belluschi office added a school and enlarged the sanctuary. The complex was again enlarged in 1952, after Belluschi had moved to the East Coast, with the addition of transepts and an extended choir loft. In 1969, to conform to the requirements of liturgical reform, the altar was pulled into the center of the crossing. These changes drastically compromised Belluschi's original concept.

shingled roof is of red cedar. The interiors, too, are of natural wood, with walls of unfinished cedar planking, sanded and burnished to a smooth sheen. The exposed structural elements create a natural, decorative, rhythmic pattern. A scissor truss made of 2-by-8 fir beams bolted together to the ridgepole spans the nave, serving, like the ribs of a Gothic vault, both a structural and decorative function. A series of supporting 2-by-4's forms a colonnade along the sides of the nave, beyond which are aisles distinguished visually and symbolically from the nave by their lower ceiling.

The altar, the most holy of liturgical sites, forms the main interior focus, which Belluschi dramatized with space and light. The nave is dim, lighted on both sides by repeated bays of diamond-leaded windows with pale-tinted cathedral glass. Against this, the chancel, defined by its raised floor and higher ceiling, is brilliantly lit by a stream of natural light from the lantern overhead. Consistent with Arts and Crafts ideals of unifying the ensemble by a consistent artistic view, Belluschi designed, or oversaw the design of, all furnishings and interior finishes—pews, baptismal font, altar railings, and lamps.

Other than the slender lancet window in the narthex, Belluschi avoided explicit religious imagery, evoking tradition instead. The por-

REFERENCES

"Saint Thomas More Chapel." *Western Building* 21, no. 4 (Apr. 1942): 6–7.

Walter Gordon. "Designed by Pietro Belluschi." *Pencil Points* 23, no. 7 (July 1942): 59–63, 75.

Church Property Administration, May – June 1945: 18–19.

"Portland, Oregon: Saint Thomas More Church." *Liturgical Arts* 17, no. 3 (May 1949): 92–93.

"The Architect and His Community: Pietro Belluschi." *Progressive Architecture* 30, no. 2 (Feb. 1949): 49.

Stubblebine, Jo, ed. *The Northwest Architecture of Pietro Belluschi* (New York: F. W. Dodge, 1953), pp. 92–93.

"Oregon: Saint Thomas Church, Portland." *Liturgical Arts* 21, no. 2 (Feb. 1953): 51.

Belluschi, Pietro. "The Churches Go Modern," Appendix.

"Additions to a Belluschi Chapel." *Architectural Record* 127, no. 3 (Mar. 1960): 32–33.

Christ-Janer, Albert, and Mary Mix Foley. *Modern Church Architecture: A Guide to the Form and Spirit of Twentieth-Century Religious Buildings* (New York: McGraw-Hill, 1962), pp. 37–39.

Taped interview, Frank Allen with author, Nov. 16, 1986 (Allen was an architect in the Doyle, then Belluschi, office in the 1930s and 1940s).

4. JUNIOR CHAPEL, FIRST METHODIST CHURCH

Alteration of an existing basement for use as a youth chapel, First Methodist Church, Portland, Oregon (1943; since demolished)
Architect: Pietro Belluschi

The project consisted of remodeling the basement of an existing parish house for use as a Sunday school chapel. Employing little more than movable partitions, indirect lighting, and bright color, Belluschi achieved the effect of a warm and intimate space despite the close quarters. To emphasize the spiritual character of the room, he used two screens of differing dimensions and contrasting woods to focus attention on the apse. The larger of the two screens, of a flush-surfaced, richly grained maple, defined the altar; the smaller, of ribbed fir, set off against the larger screen in a play of asymmetrical, overlapping planes, framed the pulpit to one side. To heighten the sense of liturgical drama, both panels were backlit, with spotlights and a simple suspended globe casting light over the altar. Belluschi brightened the windowless basement with color: dark blue-green carpet, light lemon yellow plastered walls and ceiling, and russet door and rear wall.

REFERENCES
"Problem of a Chapel: Junior Chapel, First Methodist Church, Portland, Ore." *Architectural Record* 98, no. 3 (Sept. 1945): 102.

5. CHURCH OF THE PEOPLE

Project for a small nondenominational church adjacent to the University of Washington campus, Seattle, Washington (1945)
Architect: Pietro Belluschi; design assistant: K. E. Richardson

The newly formed Church of the People wanted a structure that expressed its independence of any traditional church. The building was thus conceived as a fellowship hall in the manner of a New England meetinghouse and was governed by a spirit of international and interracial camaraderie rather than any specific sacred rite. Open to all, the building was to reflect the church's universality. Rather than relying on the talent of local architects, the congregation retained Belluschi because it was felt he understood their particular needs and was responsive to the idea of a nontraditional yet spiritual structure.

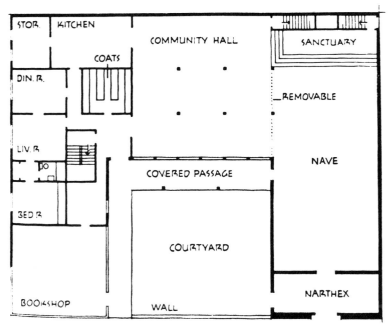

Main Floor

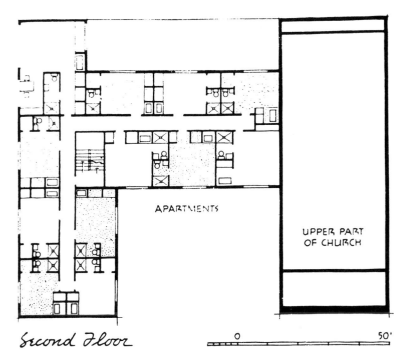

Second Floor

The site was a two-lot corner on a busy intersection across the street from the University of Washington campus in Seattle. Specific requirements called for a three-part complex of meeting hall, education-social hall, and international center. The education-social hall was to be flexible in use, providing a place for large dinners, lectures and movies, small discussion groups, and political meetings. Adjacent to the hall was to be a library and reading room. Kitchen and dining facilities were also to be included. Individual apartment units were to serve as living quarters for foreign and minority students, providing not just a place to live but a sense of home. It was hoped the building would generate an atmosphere of genuine community.

Belluschi's proposal, evidently inspired by recent work of Eero Saarinen (see fig. 10), consisted of three rectangular brick blocks of differing dimensions and fenestration patterns, grouped around a walled landscaped courtyard, which served as a private garden. Public spaces such as the main hall and bookstore were to be located at the street level, with living units above. The chapel formed one wing of the U-shaped plan, its function distinguished from the other buildings subtly by its fenestration pattern and more explicitly by the stylized sculptural group above the entrance.

Marking a clear departure from the more traditional church forms that were built before World War II, Belluschi's flat-roofed, rectilinear form, with its clean, bare surfaces and functional lines, suggests the growing influence of European modernism in the Pacific Northwest.

REFERENCES

"Church of the People, Seattle, Washington." *Progressive Architecture* 28, no. 8 (Aug. 1947): 60–61.

6. CENTRAL LUTHERAN CHURCH

Medium-sized urban church, Eugene, Oregon (1945–55)
Architect: Pietro Belluschi, completed by Belluschi/SOM

Anticipating the end of the war and needing a new church, the congregation of the Central Lutheran Church in Eugene in May 1945 commissioned Belluschi to draw up a master plan for new facilities, including a church seating five hundred, a parish hall, and administrative offices. Work on the parish house was to begin immediately so it could be used as a sanctuary until money was raised for the church. The site was a relatively large, flat lot in a quiet residential area of the city.

Belluschi pursued a direction similar to the Church of the People project of the same time (no. 5), unadorned, flat-roofed, cubical forms influenced by European modernism. Eero Saarinen's First Christian Church in Columbus, Indiana (see fig. 10), appears to have served as a point of departure.

The parish hall and offices were finished in 1947; the church itself was not built until later, after Belluschi had moved to Boston and the Portland office was managed by Belluschi/SOM. The initial concept thus was his, though the final design bears the corporate stamp.

The church consists of a simple rectangular hall, longitudinal in plan with the narthex at one end, the chancel at the other. It is sited at right angles to the parish hall, which is set back from the street to allow space for an enclosed, landscaped court and small chapel.

The exteriors are predominately dark, stained Douglas fir on a plain brick base. A simple slender cross is placed asymmetrically high above the main portal. The walls are non-loadbearing, with the roof supported internally by an independent structural framework of exposed, laminated wood.

The interior is dominated by this exposed structural framework. A series of suppressed arches divides the nave into regular bays; drawn in several feet from the exterior walls, these arches also serve as a nave arcade, defining side aisles. The chancel end is set off by its raised

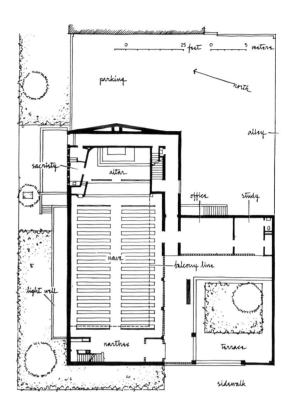

platform and a richly textured brick wall, which forms a backdrop for the altar. The nave walls are of exposed brick below and windows above of richly colored stained glass held in place by a grid of narrow wood mullions. Functioning as a clerestory, these windows shed a soft, raking light into the nave. The greatest light is reserved for the chancel, lit by a full-length window-wall of pale stained glass.

Though the basic concept dates from 1945, the church itself was not built until later in the decade and bears evidence of Belluschi's evolving ideas about design. His churches of the late 1940s, with their exposed laminated arches, richly textured brick, and stained Douglas fir screening, seem to have played a role, softening the austerity of his original design.

REFERENCES

"Building Types Study No. 229—Religious Buildings: Central Lutheran Church, Eugene, Ore." *Architectural Record* 118, no. 6 (Dec. 1955): 188–89.

"Faith's New Forms: Contemporary U.S. Churches Take on a Look of the World They Are Serving." *Life Magazine*, Dec. 26, 1955, 112.

Shear, John Knox, ed. *Religious Buildings for Today* (New York: F. W. Dodge, 1957), pp. 64–65.

Weyres, Willy, and Otto Bartning. *Kirchen Handbuch für den Kirchenbau* (Munich: Verlag Georg D. W. Callwey, 1958).

"Four Houses of Worship: Lutheran Church, Eugene, Oregon." *Progressive Architecture* 40, no. 6 (June 1959): 122–23.

7. IMMANUEL LUTHERAN CHURCH

Enlargement of a small Gothic Revival church in Silverton, Oregon (1947)
Architect: Pietro Belluschi

The Immanuel Lutheran Church in the rural town of Silverton, south of Portland, needed updating and enlarging. Specific requirements called for increasing the size of the fellowship hall, modernizing the kitchen, adding classrooms, and enhancing the overall function of the church as a community center. The congregation cherished the original white, clapboarded Gothic Revival church and wanted to retain its integrity. Respecting this desire, Belluschi minimized modification of the exterior form.

Belluschi substantially affected the character of the interior, however, by enlivening the somber gray, plastered ceiling of the nave with a brightly colored stenciled pattern. For this he drew on the gay, naturalistic motifs and ornamental flourishes of traditional Scandinavian churches. The congregation was delighted with this decorative touch, which tied in with the heritage of the Lutheran community.

Belluschi returned to the Silverton church in the 1960s for another enlargement (no. 32), then again in 1975 to design a new church (no. 36) after a fire destroyed the original building.

8. ZION LUTHERAN CHURCH

Small urban church of brick and wood, Portland, Oregon (1948–50)
Architect: Pietro Belluschi; design assistant: K. E. Richardson
Cost: $100,000

Perhaps our design will be pointed out as a compromise. Which it is, and so is our world and our society. So we offer no apology.
—Pietro Belluschi, "Notes on the Zion Lutheran Church, Portland, Oregon"

The biggest challenge Belluschi faced in this project was reconciling the congregation's expectations for a traditional church with his own principles as a modern architect. Developing a wide range of possible schemes, most of which were rejected by the congregation, Belluschi arrived at a solution that was neither ostentatiously modern nor anti-traditional. Using ordinary materials, progressive technology, a clear expression of structure and function, and a minimum of adornment, he endowed the building with a sense of timelessness. The result was not so much a compromise as a reinterpretation of traditional form in fully modern terms.

The site for the church, a corner lot several blocks from Portland's downtown, was already occupied by the congregation's traditional, white, clapboarded Gothic Revival church; this was to remain in use throughout the construction process. The new church thus had to be set back on the site to accommodate the existing structure. The old church was eventually demolished, and the area turned into a landscaped forecourt. The new church, a simple wood-frame building seating three hundred, is domestic in scale and Nordic in character. The great gabled shingle roof dominates the form, its hipped portion brought down low in front and extended beyond the narthex to form a portico supported on a slender colonnade. A spire rises from a two-tiered, square wooden cupola over the juncture of narthex and nave.

Following the slope of the site, Belluschi stepped the interior spaces upward from narthex to chancel. Each of these spatial units is

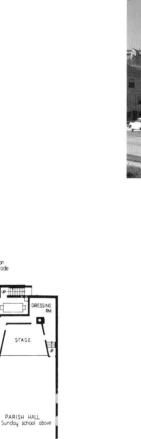

clearly expressed on the exterior: broad, projecting narthex; traditional, long, rectangular nave; set-back chancel. The progression of spaces from the narthex to chancel is given further articulation on the interior by changes in ceiling height and lighting.

The exteriors are of brick, with non-loadbearing cavity walls insulating the sanctuary from street noise. To block the view of the street and to provide privacy, Belluschi dispensed with conventional windows and instead perforated the walls with 10-inch-square glass blocks embedded into the brick; these allowed a soft, even glow of light to filter into the nave. The glass blocks are held flush on the outer surface of the wall, consistent with Belluschi's desire for a smooth exterior surface, but recessed on the interior, with the soffits lined with copper to intensify their light; directional glass was also used to cast light up into the vaults rather than down into the nave and the eyes of worshipers. Against this dimmed light in the nave, an expansive window-wall of pale rose, lavender, and amber glass, held in an abstract pattern of slender wood mullions and horizontal bars, floods the chancel with light.

The roof is carried on an internal framework of great freestanding laminated arches. In one of the earliest and most impressive postwar civilian uses of structural laminated, or glulam, timbers, they soar overhead in a series of pointed arches—a clear allusion to the Gothic ribbed vault but cast now in modern technological terms. The exposed fir ceiling is grooved to absorb sound, essential for the acoustics of the highly musical Lutheran service. Hemlock boards with redwood battens form a richly textured wall behind the altar; it, too, is acoustically absorbent to counter the hard, reflective surface of the unadorned brick walls.

A fine Willamina brick was used throughout, rosy in overall tone but of slightly varying hue to give a subtle but visually rich, textured surface. The mortar, held flush to the surface on the exterior, was pigmented to blend with the brick's color. The brick itself was set in a regular bond of straight stretchers, repeated every seven courses to introduce a subdued but consistent pattern. While suggesting the heritage of Belluschi's Italian background, more importantly it reveals his interest in contemporary trends in brickwork and his fascination with Flemish bonding patterns in particular.

Given the centrality of music in the Lutheran service, the location of the organ was crucial. Belluschi found the acoustics in church design to be a major challenge; conditions had to be responsive to both choral and organ music on the one hand and to the spoken word on the other; at the same time, inadvertent noise from the congregation had to be minimized. The acoustical problem of Zion Lutheran was exacerbated by its proximity to the street. The solution was to locate the organ at the back of the church in a choir loft above the narthex, directing and softening the quality of sound by the judicious use of sound-absorbing paneling.

The spire presented another problem. Unable to justify its presence on either structural or functional grounds, Belluschi recognized its purely symbolic purpose and profound emotional significance to the congregation. Especially young people and returning veterans felt the need for continuity with the past, and sought the reassurance provided by established symbols of faith. In a world of change and uncertainty, as Belluschi put it in his notes on the church, they needed that certainty. He questioned whether such symbols should be entirely eliminated or somehow reinvigorated in the contemporary church, concluding that "there must be a border line beyond which we cannot go, since the very essence of organized religion is one of dogmatic and symbolic thinking. This is a large field which we would not care to enter, but one which may well give us the key to the emotional demand in church architecture."

Without adornment other than the elegant metal cross over the altar and the main doors bearing a copper relief of abstracted hovering angels by the Hungarian-born artist Frederic Littman, Zion Lutheran is plain and simple. Its distinction lies in the rationality of the fully expressed structure, the subtle lighting, the natural beauty and skillful handling of the materials, and the simple directness with which Belluschi realized spiritual goals.

REFERENCES

Belluschi, Pietro. "Notes on the Zion Lutheran Church, Portland, Oregon." Undated, but ca. 1950. Unpublished manuscript, George Arents Research Library, Syracuse University.

"Church by Architect Belluschi Shows How New Techniques and Materials Can Update an Old Tradition." *Architectural Forum* 94, no. 1 (Jan. 1951): 142–46.

Priaulx, Arthur W. "Churches Can Be Different: Zion Lutheran Church." *Architect and Engineer* 189, no. 1 (Apr. 1952): 12–24.

Stubblebine, Jo, ed. *The Northwest Architecture of Pietro Belluschi* (New York: F. W. Dodge, 1953), pp. 46–47.

Thiry, Paul, Richard M. Bennett, and Henry L. Kamphoefner. *Churches and Temples* (New York: Reinhold Publishing, 1953), pp. 30P, 65P.

World's Contemporary Architecture, ed. Ino Yuichi (Tokyo: Shokokusha Publishing, 1953), vol. 2, p. 38.

Weyres, Willy, and Otto Bartning. *Kirchen Handbuch für den Kirchenbau* (Munich: Verlag Georg D. W. Callwey, 1958).

Christ-Janer, Albert, and Mary Mix Foley. *Modern Church Architecture: A Guide to the Form and Spirit of Twentieth-Century Religious Buildings* (New York: McGraw-Hill, 1962), pp. 137–45.

Taped interviews, Frank Allen with author, Nov. 16 and Dec. 6, 1986; interview, K. E. Richardson with Laura Burns Carroll, Jan. 17, 1986 (Allen and Richardson were architects in the Belluschi office who worked on the Zion Lutheran Church).

9. CENTRAL LUTHERAN CHURCH

Large urban church in Portland, Oregon (1948–50)
Architect: Pietro Belluschi; design assistant: K. E. Richardson
Cost, including parish hall and Sunday school wing: $250,000

"A church is individual for each congregation, not just a shelter. You have to create an emotional feeling with materials, the funds available, and our own knowledge of today's architecture," Belluschi told the congregation of Central Lutheran Church. Refusing at the outset to design a church in the Gothic style, he explained: "I do not want to be different; I want to be in the same tradition as the people who designed Gothic churches. The trouble is we are not in the Gothic age." Using the architectural forms and techniques of the postwar era, Belluschi provided the Lutheran congregation with a building fully of its time yet consistent with the spirit of the past.

The site was a large, flat corner lot in a middle-class residential area of Portland. As the program called for a wide range of facilities in a limited space—fellowship hall, parish hall, administrative offices, and Sunday school, in addition to the sanctuary—it demanded the utmost in efficient planning. The church was bounded on two sides by busy streets with little room for a buffer; thus noise and visual privacy were important factors. Another challenge was to provide an appropriately scaled sanctuary, capable of handling a congregation of one thousand without overwhelming the residential setting. But even in this, his largest church to date, Belluschi sought to create a quiet, meditative space.

Reflecting his interest in both Japanese architecture and the current work of Alvar Aalto, Belluschi used nontraditional forms of warm, textured brick combined with an open framework of dark stained wood. The plan and general massing were traditional, with a simple longitudinal nave, a broad narthex at one end and a raised chancel with semicircular apse at the other, and a single open timberwork tower flanking the narthex.

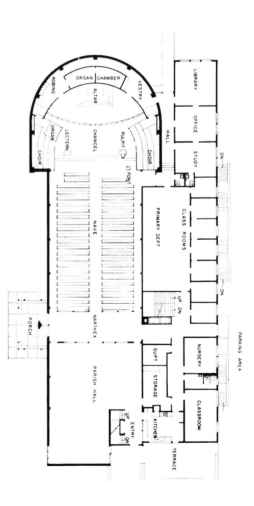

There tradition stopped. Rather than on axis, the entrance is at right angles, defined by a curve-roofed Japanese wooden gate, which opens onto the broad, shallow narthex. From here one can proceed into either a fellowship hall to the right or the nave to the left. Enclosed on both sides by movable panels, the narthex can be opened up, expanding the nave to the full length of the building on holidays and other special occasions.

The chancel is both wider and taller than the nave, so that a vertical glazed zone between the two provides a halo of light around the altar. The nave is lit on the street side by high stained-glass windows held in a wooden grid; in hues ranging from pale blues to saturated reds and purples, the windows fill the nave with a richly colored but subdued light, providing a dramatic contrast to the chancel, which is brilliantly lit by its halo of natural light. Opposite the stained glass, the inner nave wall is of vertical, stained-wood battens backed by an acoustical, sound-absorbing fabric. A similar screen is used behind the altar.

Spanning the nave are six great, suppressed laminated arches. Unlike the considerably smaller Zion Lutheran Church, where the arches are freestanding, drawn in about 3 feet from the peripheral wall on either side to form side aisles, here they are embedded in the nave walls and span the full 44-foot-wide nave. In contrast to the nave with its richly textured walls, the chancel is defined by a plain, flat plaster wall originally painted a soft blue to symbolize the sky according to Lutheran custom.

Central Lutheran suggests a mingling of Japanese and Nordic traditions, reminding one of the commonalities in cultural traditions of Scandinavia, the Far East, and the Pacific Northwest. The brick exteriors, given a distinctive, densely textured bond of repeated recessed crosses, recall those of Alvar Aalto, while the curve-roofed gateway, the modularity of the nave elevation, and the exposed timberwork construction are all Japanese in feeling.

Commissioned in 1945, the design of Central Lutheran went through a number of stages, including one scheme of reinforced concrete. The church was not completed until 1951, after Belluschi had moved east.

The exterior wood framing, originally stained a soft brown to blend with the earthy tones of the warm brick, was later painted black. It has now been restored to its original color. The lighting of the chancel has also been changed to reduce glare.

REFERENCES

"Central Lutheran Church." *Construction News Bulletin* (Mar. 17, 1951): 8–10.

"Modern Gothic in Wood." *Architectural Forum* 95, no. 6 (Dec. 1951): 163–67.

Stubblebine, Jo, ed. *The Northwest Architecture of Pietro Belluschi* (New York: F. W. Dodge, 1953), pp. 48–51.

Thiry, Paul, Richard M. Bennett, and Henry L. Kamphoefner. *Churches and Temples* (New York: Reinhold Publishing, 1953), pp. 52P–53P.

"One Hundred Years of Significant Building, 7: Churches (Central Lutheran Church, Portland, 1951)." *Architectural Record* 120, no. 6 (Dec. 1956): 177–80.

Weyres, Willy, and Otto Bartning. *Kirchen Handbuch für den Kirchenbau* (Munich: Verlag Georg D. W. Callwey, 1958).

Hosfield, John David. "Study of the Architecture of Pietro Belluschi: 1925–1950." M.A. thesis, University of Oregon, 1960, pp. 62–63.

Christ-Janer, Albert, and Mary Mix Foley. *Modern Church Architecture: A Guide to the Form and Spirit of Twentieth-Century Religious Buildings* (New York: McGraw-Hill, 1962), p. 144.

Hayes, Bartlett. *Tradition Becomes Innovation: Modern Religious Architecture in America* (New York: Pilgrim Press, 1983), p. 56.

Taped interview, Frank Allen with author, Dec. 6, 1986 (Allen was an architect in the Belluschi office involved in the design development of Central Lutheran).

10. ST. PHILIP NERI CATHOLIC CHURCH

Large urban Catholic church in Portland, Oregon (1946–52)
Architect: Pietro Belluschi; design assistant: Walter Gordon
Cost: $250,000

The Italian congregation of the Catholic church of St. Philip Neri wanted a building recalling the old churches of their native land. Commissioned in December 1945, the project had an exceptionally tight budget and was prolonged by fund-raising problems. Although preliminary studies were begun in January 1946, final plans were not approved until March 1947, and then construction was put off, while cost estimates rose sharply. After severe cost-cutting measures were taken, construction was begun in the fall of 1949. Still unfinished, the bare-bones concrete building was dedicated in October 1950, without its brick veneer. The building was completed in 1952, well after Belluschi had left for MIT.

Belluschi's principal aim was to keep the design as simple and economical as possible. In keeping with the congregation's desires, he used an Early Christian brick basilica as a prototype. As an adaptation of a common Roman secular building type, the Early Christian church was a plain hall for the assembly of large numbers of people, and thus very different in character from the more costly, elaborate, and richly adorned cathedral of the later Gothic era. The site was flat and bare, in a lower-middle-class residential neighborhood in east Portland filled mostly with wooden bungalows.

A large, unadorned building of variegated brick, stark and imposing in scale, Philip Neri clearly conveys its religious purpose despite lacking the customary trappings of the conventional, historicized church. The disposition of spaces—rectangular transept-less nave with side aisles and narthex, flat chancel end, semicircular baptistry to one side of the entrance, and freestanding bell tower to the other—is clearly legible on the exterior. The fenestration makes explicit the nature of the interior spaces: great rose window over the narthex; series of tall, narrow, slit windows defining bays of the nave; expansive window-wall of pale stained glass in the chancel end.

The interior is equally straightforward. One enters on axis, as was customary in the traditional basilica, through a narthex, which also serves as an overflow space, into the nave. The nave itself consists of a high volume of space defined by plain plaster walls carried on a series of blunt, square pillars; beyond these are aisles defined by their lower ceilings. Relieving the severity of the flush-surfaced interior but serving primarily an acoustical purpose, almost imperceptible pleats, one per bay, zigzag gently along the nave wall. An exposed timber roof vaults the nave, as in the Early Christian basilica, supported on clear-span beams forming a series of low triangular trusses. A simple arched canopy of wood originally framed the altar. The structure was of reinforced concrete with exteriors of a buff-colored Willamina brick in a richly textured bond.

Most of the present interior decoration was added later, including the elaborate baldachino.

REFERENCES

Priaulx, Arthur W. "Churches in the Modern Mood." *Architect and Engineer* 195, no. 3 (Dec. 1953): 17, 21–22.

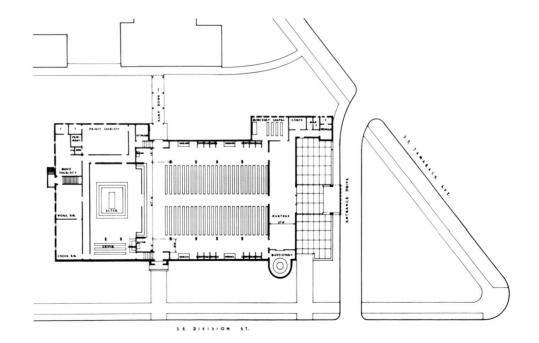

11. FIRST PRESBYTERIAN CHURCH

Neighborhood church in Cottage Grove, Oregon (1948–51)
Architect: Pietro Belluschi; design assistant: K. E. Richardson
Cost: $126,000

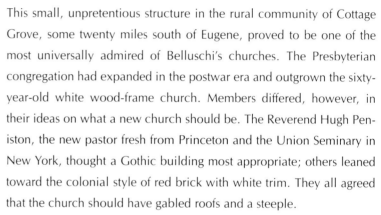

To those who understand the quiet harmony of nature.
—Samuel Newsom, *Japanese Garden Construction*

This small, unpretentious structure in the rural community of Cottage Grove, some twenty miles south of Eugene, proved to be one of the most universally admired of Belluschi's churches. The Presbyterian congregation had expanded in the postwar era and outgrown the sixty-year-old white wood-frame church. Members differed, however, in their ideas on what a new church should be. The Reverend Hugh Peniston, the new pastor fresh from Princeton and the Union Seminary in New York, thought a Gothic building most appropriate; others leaned toward the colonial style of red brick with white trim. They all agreed that the church should have gabled roofs and a steeple.

Because of the differing opinions, the congregation postponed making a decision, and Peniston himself went to the School of Architecture library at the University of Oregon to learn about current trends in church design. The congregation and pastor decided they did not want a conventional, status-asserting edifice but something more natural, built of the materials and utilizing the skills of the local community, whose main industry was lumber, and tailored to their particular needs. Though there were more accessible architects, Belluschi was appealing because of his views on the use of native materials and natural light, his idea of a graduated approach from street to sanctuary, and his overall philosophy of architectural design: to build simply, rationally, economically, and without pretension.

The site was a corner lot bordered by one-hundred-year-old honey locust trees in a quiet residential neighborhood. Preserving the trees was one of the stipulations presented to Belluschi, as the lot had been donated by a member of the congregation whose parents had

brought the honey locust seeds to Oregon in the 1850s. This proviso delighted Belluschi, given his concern for the natural landscape, though it complicated site planning, already challenging because of the confining lot and amount of space required. The job called for a parish hall, kitchen, Sunday school classrooms, nursery, library, and administrative offices, in addition to the sanctuary. Most important, however, was the desire for a spiritual space, both intimate and inspiring, a place of refuge for private devotion as well as communal worship. That Belluschi would use wood, the economic lifeblood of the community and source of income for the principal donors, was understood.

In keeping with the Presbyterian tradition and its denial of papal authority expressed architecturally with a segregated altar in a special sanctified space, the communion table was to form the nucleus of a single, undivided interior. The choir, rather than being located in the chancel behind the minister or in a balcony in back of the nave, was to be to one side so that all participants in the service—minister, congregation, and members of the choir—would be grouped around the table as a single, united family gathered at a communal meal. Pastor Peniston had also heard of a church in Scotland rebuilt after the war so that one looked out a clear expanse of glass beyond the communion table onto the slums of Glasgow and the broader community to which the church was responsible. Belluschi responded by designing a nave fully opened along one side through a series of clear plate-glass windows. From the sanctuary one could look onto an enclosed garden, with the view of the street blocked by a trellised fence but over which were visible the rooftops of houses and the surrounding community.

As this was Belluschi's first Presbyterian church, he learned as much as he could about the denomination's needs. He pounded the congregation with questions—about its tradition, liturgy, and values—and was given background literature. By the time he and his design assistant, K. E. Richardson, started the design process, they were fully informed on the needs of the church. Some seven different floor plans were proposed, each rejected or revised on the basis of comments from the congregation. One of the women suggested facilitating access by reversing the orientation of the sanctuary so the chancel faced west rather than east, an idea that made eminent sense to Belluschi. The same woman planned the kitchen, proving to be a much better re-

source, in Belluschi's eyes, than the professionals he had intended to use. His receptivity to suggestions, however humble their source, so contrary to the legendary arrogance of the celebrated architect, was one of Belluschi's remarkable characteristics that not only endeared him to clients and coworkers but added immeasurably to the overall richness and success of the work.

Not until the plan was approved did Belluschi turn to the elevation. He had consistently steered the congregation away from thinking about the exterior form or how the building would look. More important was to determine the disposition of spaces, a good functional plan, and then to let the exterior follow.

By the time a model was prepared, the congregation was fully abreast of current trends in church design. Nonetheless, Belluschi's scheme stunned them, and members of the building committee were not sure they liked it. At Belluschi's suggestion, however, they agreed to give it time. After studying the model and thinking about it in light of all their requirements, they reconvened. "I don't really like it," was the comment of one woman, "but when you think of it, Mr. Belluschi has done exactly what we asked him to. The plan expresses simply those ideas we wanted expressed." Hearing that, proponents knew the battle was won: Belluschi's logic was clear.

The solution was a modest structure of wood, set back on the lot to preserve the cluster of trees. The horizontal form of the church, gently undulating up over the chancel and indicating its importance, reached out to the community, rejecting a soaring Gothic verticality expressive of otherworldliness, and echoing the social values of the Cottage Grove congregation. The church's exteriors of rough wood, stained to match the bark of the locust trees, conveyed the sense of naturalness the congregation sought, a symbolic as well as visual fit into the community and the integration with the natural environment that comprised their world.

Belluschi's skill in site planning was matched by his handling of the circulation. Setting the L-shaped building back on the site allowed room for a secluded Japanese landscaped garden to be tucked into the angle; screened by a discreet trellised fence, the small but spacious-seeming garden provided a psychological and emotional transition between the street and church. Entering through a wooden gateway, one

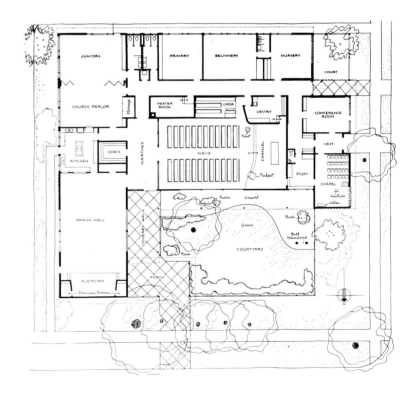

opposite wall. To absorb sound, grooved decking on the back wall and ceiling was used at the suggestion of Frank Allen, one of the architects in the Belluschi office who had originally suggested the use of fir decking in Zion Lutheran (no. 8). The continuous floor-to-ceiling glazing of the nave wall along the garden side eliminated any sense of barrier between interior and exterior, enclosed sanctuary and open landscape, the society of others and the solitude of nature. As with Central Lutheran (no. 9), the church represented a merging of East and West, of Japanese spirituality and Western materialism, and a harmony of building and garden.

The nave and chancel were conceived as a single space, with the choir loft and organ to one side. On the chancel wall above the communion table is a simple wooden cross, painted the same shade of white as the wall and rendered visible by subtle lighting and shadow rather than color. It is one of the few explicit religious symbols in the church, along with the baptismal font and carved wooden campanile in the garden.

The campanile posed a problem. Belluschi had initially opposed it, believing it to be an unnecessary vestige of the traditional church. He informed Pastor Peniston in a letter that they were having difficulty finding a form for the campanile that fit the design scheme; moreover, he argued, the skilled wood-carvers needed to carve it would be hard to find. When Peniston replied that the bell played an important role in the service and was rung every Sunday, Belluschi realized its significance and responded immediately with a design. Peniston carved the campanile himself.

In describing his concept for the church and its garden, Belluschi had suggested the use of natural rocks, which play an important role in Japanese landscaping. He told the congregation of the time often spent finding a rock with just the right size and shape, and the care with which each stone was placed in a precise pattern, leading visitors through a garden as they mentally prepared for the experience ahead. Belluschi envisioned a large rock at the entrance which would cause visitors to pivot upon entering the gate, directing them down the sheltered path to the narthex. It would also screen the sanctuary, fully glazed on this side, from public view. He had spotted a large boulder he thought might be suitable in a quarry in Idaho. It had been cut,

proceeds to the narthex down a path bordering the enclosed garden; pivoting to the right, the visitor enters the nave, whose axis parallels the garden and terminates in the communion table, the focal point of the plan. Belluschi's aim was to create a series of visual and spiritual discoveries as one progressed in time and space through the various parts of the church.

The nave itself is simple, spare, and, like the garden, small but seemingly spacious. Plain, white, sand-plastered walls were used in the chancel and along one side; vertically grained fir decking, treated only with a light lacquer to allow it to age naturally, was used on the however, into a regular rectangular block and bore all the mechanical tool marks of quarrying; moreover, the cost of transporting it would be high. Under the circumstances, he suggested using a simple lattice instead. Smitten by his original idea, members of the congregation looked on their own and found a naturally sculpted stone that seemed perfect. One of the maintenance men of the church, who was also a member of the congregation, suggested they haul it to the site themselves. The rock became a key element in the total design, a Zen touch of the serendipitous. Zen, however, was not part of their thinking. Belluschi was drawn to Japanese landscape design not for its philosophy but for its economy, serenity, visual order, and most of all for its naturalness and sense of oneness with nature.

One of the most highly respected of Belluschi's early Pacific Northwest churches, the Cottage Grove Presbyterian Church, offering spiritual refuge at once intimate, inspirational, and universal in its appeal, proved a classic. Its success was due in large measure to Belluschi's ability to listen, his openness to the suggestions of others, and his respect for their views. Peniston explained the process as educational for them all: "Belluschi was amazingly responsive to our ideas, and persuasive in helping us to understand his. It is hard for me to explain the excitement we all felt. You have to understand something of the atmosphere that prevailed in the Belluschi organization, as well as the feeling in our congregation that our little church was about to do something new."

Belluschi himself described the process as one of mutual learning: "I was trying to understand their theory and they were trying to understand mine." He found the Cottage Grove Presbyterian congregation a small, close-knit community "where the real religion is in the sense of a loving community, of being, helping each other. That was the strength of it. That is why the small church *means* so much more, even if you are not religious. There was a sense of community throughout. It was really a process of understanding, and being a part of it." Because of this empathy, he was able to visualize and express the congregation's traditions, values, and spiritual aspirations so successfully in architectural form.

United by a common sense of purpose, Belluschi and his chief designer, K. E. Richardson, Peniston, the building committee, congregation, and contractor all worked closely together. While the fir decking was being nailed to the ceiling, the contractor, a skilled craftsman of Norwegian heritage, called up to the carpenters to watch each hammer blow to avoid misses. The carpenters laughed, replying that no one would be able to detect an errant hammer mark up there. The contractor's response was firm: he would know it was there, and there were to be no flaws in his church. This pride and sense of individual involvement, this shared concern for quality—much of it inspired by Belluschi—contributed immeasurably to the building's success.

The First Presbyterian Church represented an entirely fresh approach to the design of the church. This new architectural expression that captured the traditional spirit of a house of worship attested Belluschi's deep understanding of the spiritual needs of the modern age. The oldest member of the congregation spoke for many when she said, "I was fond of the old church. But I feel closer to God in the new one."

REFERENCES

"1951 Design Survey, Religion: Churches, First Presbyterian Church, Cottage Grove, Oregon." *Progressive Architecture* 32, no. 1 (Jan. 1951): 75.

"First Presbyterian Church, Cottage Grove, Oregon." *Progressive Architecture* 33, no. 3 (Mar. 1952): 63–67.

Stubblebine, Jo, ed. *The Northwest Architecture of Pietro Belluschi* (New York: F. W. Dodge, 1953), pp. 52–55.

World's Contemporary Architecture, ed. Ino Yuichi (Tokyo: Shokokusha Publishing, 1953), vol. 3, p. 50.

Hitchcock, Henry-Russell. *Architecture: Nineteenth and Twentieth Centuries* (Harmondsworth, Middlesex, England: Penguin Books Ltd., 1958), p. 422.

Peter, John. *Masters of Modern Architecture* (New York: George Braziller, 1958), p. 170.

Christ-Janer, Albert, and Mary Mix Foley. *Modern Church Architecture: A Guide to the Form and Spirit of Twentieth-Century Religious Buildings* (New York: McGraw-Hill, 1962), pp. 207–14.

Kidder Smith, G. E. *A Pictorial History of Architecture in America* (New York: American Heritage Publishing Co., 1976), p. 774.

Taped interviews, Belluschi with author, Aug. 12, 1988; Rev. Hugh Peniston with author, May 19, 1990.

MIDDLE CHURCHES,
EAST COAST, MIDWEST, WEST COAST

12. FIRST LUTHERAN CHURCH

Small urban church in Boston, Massachusetts (1955–57)
Architect: Pietro Belluschi; design assistant: George Wallace
Cost: $250,000

For this, his first church in the East, Belluschi was asked to design a new building that would seat three hundred in a modern idiom that would not be out of character with the other buildings in Boston's historic Back Bay. The site was tight, on the corner of a busy intersection opposite the First Church of Boston (1860s). The budget was $269,000, which seemed substantial at first but proved to be unexpectedly constricting, since Belluschi was unprepared for both the high building costs on the East Coast and the marshy soil of the Back Bay, which necessitated special pilings. Building restrictions were also very different from those in Portland.

The biggest challenge Belluschi faced in the Boston project, however, arose from the change in his architectural practice. No longer the head of his own office as he had been in Portland, Belluschi was now functioning independently as a design consultant in association with local architectural firms. This meant he no longer had a team of co-workers whom he had selected and trained, who knew his formal language and respected his architectural values. In this instance, because the job was small and the site just several blocks from his home, Belluschi worked directly with contractors, relying on the assistance of George Wallace, a former staff member who had followed him to Boston from his Portland office. After months of trying out dozens of different designs, finally, with the use of new structural systems developed at MIT, they arrived at a simple rectangular, brick form, longitudinal in plan, with a thin, barrel-vault concrete shell roof carried on steel columns embedded in non-loadbearing brick walls.

Following a by-now-characteristic progression of spaces, the visitor approaches the church through a trellised gateway on one side leading into a private, landscaped courtyard, then turns at an angle into a narrow narthex, and from there enters the nave. The sanctuary is lit by

a continuous zone of clear glass forming a clerestory just below the eaves. The greatest amount of illumination was saved for the chancel, lit by a broad window-wall of stained glass facing the private garden. Both interior and exterior walls are of exposed brick, the color and texture of which Belluschi carefully selected. A series of brick perforations tightly clustered in groups of six flank and articulate the bearing columns. Slatted wood screens backed by a sound-absorbing material at both the front and back of the nave add texture while controlling acoustics. Despite the change in formal language from his earlier regional work in the Pacific Northwest, Belluschi's approach was basically as before: a clear, rational structural system and ordinary materials, skillfully handled to enhance their natural beauty. Other than a plain metal cross over the altar and the stained glass, the building is unadorned.

A choir loft above the narthex provides additional seating. Offices and a pastor's study are located in a wing at right angles to the church, facing the secluded garden court. Sunday school, kitchen, and other facilities are on the floor below.

Belluschi admitted that in his quest for simplicity the exteriors were perhaps too severe. He had originally envisioned the principal facade as a backdrop for a major abstract sculpture; the congregation rejected the idea, however, feeling he had gone far enough in the direction of modern abstraction, and a simple granite slab bearing an inscription was used instead.

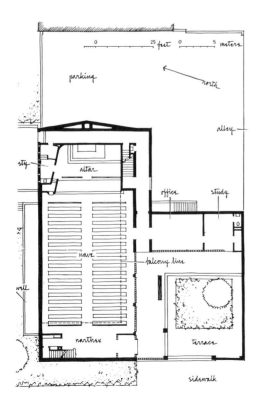

REFERENCES

Hudnut, Joseph. "The Church in a Modern World." *Architectural Forum* 109, no. 6 (Dec. 1958): 89–90.

Newman, Robert B. "Every Building Has Acoustical Problems." *Progressive Architecture* 40, no. 5 (May 1959): 156–57.

"Four Houses of Worship (Lutheran Church, Boston)." *Progressive Architecture* 40, no. 6 (June 1959): 114–17.

Goody, Joan E. *New Architecture in Boston* (Cambridge, Mass.: MIT Press, 1965), pp. 64–65.

Mutrux, Robert H. *Great New England Churches: Sixty-five Houses of Worship That Changed Our Lives* (Chester, Conn.: Globe Pequot Press, 1982), pp. 35–38.

Clausen, Meredith L. "Transparent Structure: Belluschi Churches of the 1950s." *Faith and Form* 24 (Fall 1990): 10–14.

13. PORTSMOUTH ABBEY CHURCH

Small church and monastery for a private Benedictine school, Portsmouth, Rhode Island (commissioned 1952; revised plans 1957; finished 1961)
Architect: Pietro Belluschi; associated architects: Anderson, Beckwith & Haible

Thoughtful architects have always been concerned with the environment. At their best, they have searched for reality and tried, not always successfully, to recapture and strengthen the ties that bind man to the natural order of things. In view of the spreading urban and industrial blight, this concern has now become universal and pressing. We realize with a deepening sense of sorrow that our responses are mostly secondhand, provided by the mass media in world-wide uniformity. We have grown more and more away from nature and from the discipline which nature requires. We travel at the speed of sound and see everything but experience too little. The difficult task of re-establishing a more humane world should be one of the goals of the educational process, which is best applied in the early years of a child's life, when knowledge is turning into awareness and the whole range of feelings open up to become lifelong values and the measure of one's worth. Society is undergoing great changes, particularly in the enlarged scale of space and time; but we cannot forget that the individual remains physiologically unchanged, that his basic emotions cannot be denied, that love of color and texture and play of light have real meaning to him and that merely intellectual rationalizations will not satisfy him for long.

—Pietro Belluschi, *Portsmouth Abbey School Fall Bulletin*

The Portsmouth Abbey, a preparatory school founded in 1918 by Benedictine monks, lacked a monastery and permanent church. Located on 118 acres amid the gently rolling hills and pastures of the Portsmouth Peninsula overlooking Narragansett Bay, the school had, over the years, acquired an assemblage of farm and school buildings, among them an imposing white, clapboarded Queen Anne manor house of 1863 by the architect Richard Upjohn; a gabled, brick, collegiate Gothic building of 1930; and student dormitories and a gymnasium built in the 1940s by the Boston firm of Anderson/Beckwith (later Anderson, Beckwith & Haible). In the spring of 1952, Belluschi was contacted about the design of a new church and monastery.

The client sought a building that was distinctly modern but had more warmth than was usually offered by the European modernism then dominating East Coast schools of architecture. Intended to blend harmoniously with the natural landscape, the church was to function as a place for the daily private worship of some twenty-five to thirty monks and for regular Sunday services for the entire student body. Seating capacity was to be three hundred.

Belluschi's initial scheme, part of his long-range master plan for the whole campus, consisted of a U-shaped complex with church on one side, refectory on the other, and a smaller monastery with its own enclosed court or monastic garden forming the wing in between. The church itself was to have been longitudinal in plan, a simple, low-profile structure, with fieldstone exteriors and a barrel-vault shell roof with flared overhanging eaves, a cupola, and a spire over the raised choir end. The thin, gently undulating concrete roof was to have been carried on freestanding laminated arches running the length of the

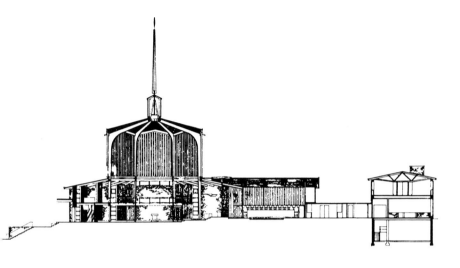

nave, with their direction turned to run crosswise at the chancel end. The walls of the nave were to be built of solid fieldstone up to the clerestory level, with tinted glass above held in a continuous wooden grille. In contrast, the chancel was to have been fully lit by an expansive stained-glass window on the north side. As the centerpiece of the design, Belluschi envisioned a fresco or mural of soaring angels painted overhead in the apse.

The project was delayed for several years, during which time the client's thinking changed. It was felt that the church should be higher, dominating the abbey complex. A centralized rather than a longitudinal plan was proposed, and the octagonal martyrium of San Vitale, Ravenna, was mentioned as a possible prototype; the octagonal form, which would allow individual radiating chapels on each of the eight sides, seemed especially well suited to a monastic order. By this time Belluschi was involved in the design of another centralized polygonal structure, the Swampscott, Massachusetts, synagogue (no. 14).

Revised plans of 1957 show the building as it was eventually built. Sited on the rise of a hill overlooking the rest of the campus, the church is composed of a series of structurally articulated, graduated octagons, the principal one forming a two-story sanctuary with a gallery on the upper level; above this rises a smaller eight-sided dome, then a still smaller octagonal cupola surmounted by a tall slender spire. The outer walls of the sanctuary consist of non-loadbearing convex slabs of local fieldstone alternating with concave panels of stained redwood, with slit windows between. Above them the dome is supported on an independent, fully exposed internal framework of radiating laminated bents. The nave is lit primarily by light from the dome, all eight sides of which are glazed with brilliant, saturated colored glass held in place by a redwood grille.

The centerpiece of the church, suspended over the altar, is a sculpture of fine wire filaments by the New York abstract artist Richard Lippold. Radiating into the space of the nave, the thin wire threads shoot light outward from a discrete skylight overhead while also funneling it down onto the altar. The sculpture thus pursues the same theme of light and space as the architecture itself, enhancing its symbolism and sacred meaning. This and a tapestry over the altar of the Holy Virgin, by Esther Puccinelli, are the only ornament.

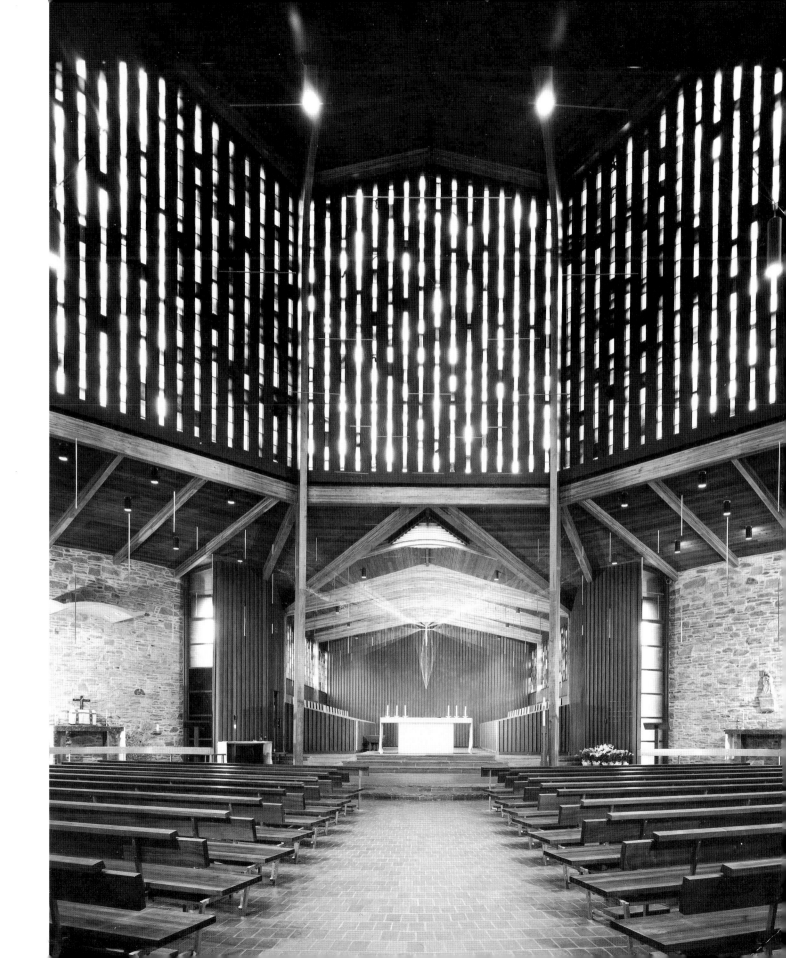

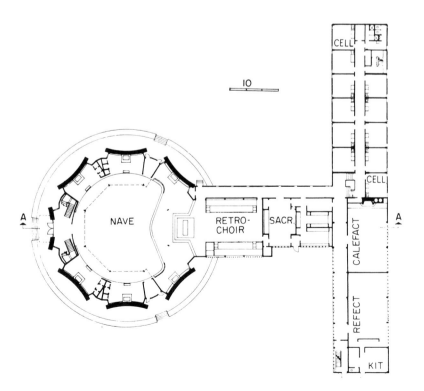

CELL

10

CELL

NAVE

RETRO-
CHOIR

SACR.

CALEFACT

A

A

REFECT

KIT

REFERENCES

"Monastery for the Portsmouth Priory." *Architectural Record* 116, no. 6 (Dec. 1954): 140–42.

"Building Types Study No. 272: Pietro Belluschi: Church and Monastery for Portsmouth Priory." *Architectural Record* 126, no. 1 (July 1959): 148–53.

"The New Churches." *Time Magazine*, Dec. 26, 1960, 28–33.

"Belluschi Designs a Church and Monastery for Portsmouth Priory." *Architectural Record* 129, no. 7 (June 1961): 116–21.

Stead, Julian. "Le Prieuré Saint-Grégoire à Portsmouth." *Art d'église* (Oct. – Dec. 1961): 118–20.

Christ-Janer, Albert, and Mary Mix Foley. *Modern Church Architecture: A Guide to the Form and Spirit of Twentieth-Century Religious Buildings* (New York: McGraw-Hill, 1962), pp. 301–7.

"Priory of Saint Gregory the Great, Portsmouth, R.I." *Liturgical Arts* 31, no. 2 (Feb. 1963): 48–52.

Mazmanian, Arthur B. *The Structure of Praise: A Design Study: Architecture for Religion in New England from the Seventeenth Century to the Present* (Boston: Beacon Press, 1970), pp. 24–28.

Belluschi, Pietro. "Some Thoughts on the Architecture of Portsmouth Abbey." *Portsmouth Abbey School Fall Bulletin* (1971).

Mutrux, Robert H. *Great New England Churches: Sixty-five Houses of Worship That Changed Our Lives* (Chester, Conn.: Globe Pequot Press, 1982), pp. 130–33.

Hayes, Bartlett. *Tradition Becomes Innovation: Modern Religious Architecture in America* (New York: Pilgrim Press, 1983), p. 73.

Tillich, Paul. *On Art and Architecture*, ed. John Dillenberger and Jane Dillenberger (New York: Crossroad Publishing Co., 1987), pp. 193, 227.

Taped interviews: Lawrence B. Anderson with author, Mar. 23, 1989, and Apr. 2, 1989; Father Peter Sidler of Portsmouth Abbey with author, Apr. 1, 1989; Robert Brannen with author, Apr. 6, 1989 (Brannen worked as Belluschi's assistant on this project).

Clausen, Meredith L. "Transparent Structure: Belluschi Churches of the 1950s." *Faith and Form* 24 (Fall 1990): 10–14.

An interest in Zen Buddhism pervaded much of the thinking at Portsmouth and resulted in the inclusion of a Zen garden, designed and laid out by one of the fathers. Although sympathetic to the spirit of Zen and familiar with Japanese design principles, Belluschi himself was perhaps more affected by the theologian Paul Tillich, who, in challenging the role of traditional symbols in modern religious architecture, proposed "sacred emptiness" as an appropriate modern alternative. This, according to Tillich, was "not an emptiness by privation, but an emptiness by inspiration. It is not an emptiness where we feel empty, but an emptiness where we feel the empty space is filled with the presence of that which cannot be expressed in any finite form."

14. TEMPLE ISRAEL

Synagogue in Swampscott, Massachusetts (1953–56)
Architect: Pietro Belluschi; design assistant: George Wallace;
associates: Carl Koch & Associates; project architect: Leon Lipshutz
Cost, exclusive of landscaping and furnishings: $600,000

Temple Israel was Belluschi's first synagogue. As the Jewish temple had no generally accepted, time-honored architectural prototype, Belluschi was free to develop the design however he wanted. The only major requirement was a flexible plan providing seating for two hundred fifty people on a regular basis yet capable of expanding to accommodate the entire congregation of eleven to eighteen hundred on High Holidays. A second factor was the existing substructure of a former synagogue building that had been begun, then abandoned. The site was ideal, a flat, spacious lot in an affluent, richly landscaped residential area.

The concept of a domed hexagonal space for the sanctuary that could open up by means of partitions into a larger rectangular hall was suggested by Carl Koch, Belluschi's associate, while Belluschi himself was abroad. Recognizing its merit, Belluschi translated the basic concept into his own formal language. The results were new in Belluschi's work but reflect his personal, rationalized approach to architectural design, with an explicit structural framework of steel and laminated wood beams, richly textured brickwork, and stained redwood. Simple in form, monumental in aspect, yet human in scale, with visual appeal derived solely from the skillful use of straightforward brick, wood, and stained glass in lieu of applied decoration, Temple Israel exerts a quiet distinction appropriate for its place and purpose.

Instead of the subdued light and contemplative space appropriate for a Protestant or Catholic church, ample light was needed in the synagogue for the reading of the Torah, the core of the Jewish service. Belluschi accomplished this by fully glazing the sides of the 40-foot-high hexagonal dome with a translucent tinted glass, reserving clear glass for the six-sided oculus in the dome overhead.

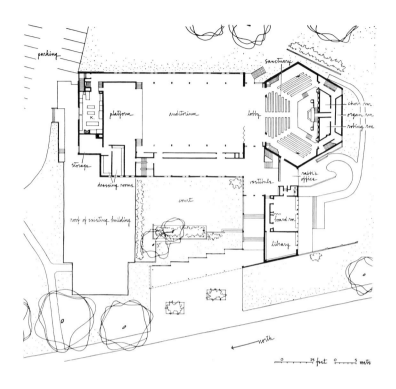

At the apex of the flat-sided dome is an open hexagonal structure serving as a cupola, surmounted by a small, slender spire and a Star of David, the only traditional symbol used in the building.

Below the sanctuary is a small chapel for weddings and other special occasions. Classrooms, stage space, a kitchen, and other subsidiary spaces are also below grade, incorporated into the existing substructure of the former building.

REFERENCES

"Alterations and Additions to Temple Israel." *Architectural Record* 116, no. 6 (Dec. 1954): 143–45.

"Four Houses of Worship (Synagogue, Swampscott/Marblehead, Massachusetts)." *Progressive Architecture* 40, no. 6 (June 1959): 124–29.

"Swampscott Churches—Temple Israel." *Daily Evening News* [Lynn, Mass.], Nov. 11, 1959.

Clausen, Meredith L. "Transparent Structure: Belluschi Churches of the 1950s." *Faith and Form* 24 (Fall 1990): 10–14.

15. TEMPLE ADATH ISRAEL

Synagogue in Merion, Pennsylvania, a suburban community
outside Philadelphia (1956–59)
Architect: Pietro Belluschi; associate: Charles Frederick Wise
Cost, including landscaping and furnishings: $754,790

The commission called for adding a fourteen-hundred-seat sanctuary to a recently completed, undistinguished L-shaped education and administration building. The site was accommodating: spacious and flat, in a well-to-do residential area west of Philadelphia.

Belluschi designed the synagogue in the form of a compact polygonal building tucked into the angle of the L to partially obscure the original building and to free the rest of the site for landscaping and parking. The plan also preserved most of the old, beautiful trees, one of Belluschi's primary site-planning concerns.

Belluschi's main objective was a clearly legible structural system. His original scheme called for a twelve-sided steel structure bearing on a compression ring in the center above which rose a smaller twelve-sided cupola with stained-glass sides. The walls of the sanctuary consisted of non-loadbearing, gently bowed, freestanding panels of brick between exposed structural steel members. In the final version, a less expensive framed system of poured concrete was used instead of steel.

The effect was of a lightweight tent screening a space rather than a walled enclosure. Though Belluschi maintains it was unintended, his concept of a lightweight, tentlike structure meshed with the traditional Judaic notion of the first synagogue, Moses's Tent of Meeting. The twelve-sided form also alluded to the Twelve Tribes of Israel.

On the interior, the hard, reflective surfaces of the brick walls and concrete roof, plus the nearly circular plan, posed new acoustical problems for which Belluschi enlisted the assistance of acousticians Bolt Berancek & Newman. A small, shallow, two-row balcony had to be added to accommodate additional seating; this was cantilevered out from the peripheral wall, obviating the need for supporting columns that would have blocked sight lines. The balcony also provided a gradation between the low-ceilinged peripheral aisle and the high vault of the main sanctuary space.

The tall twelve-sided dome was glazed with 7-foot-high sections of deep red and blue stained glass held in a filigree framework of lead cames. Glazing throughout the rest of the building was of cathedral glass, except for the narrow panels of transparent glass on either side of the structural columns. This glass framing emphasized the delicacy of the slender structural system.

Though there was no historically sanctioned architectural form for the Jewish synagogue, its form had been traditionally based on the concept of a place for spiritual study and prayer rather than a house of God. Finding a convincing way to express this was not easy, Belluschi admitted. Relying on a clearly stated structural system, simple but of the right proportions, he felt was the most appropriate way to give the building lasting meaning and beauty.

Belluschi was never fully satisfied with the outcome, especially the interior structural brace forming the Star of David at the base of the dome, which he found ponderous, mitigating the effect of a lightweight cage. But as the brace served a structural purpose, removing it would have entailed a major design revision. The color of the glazing in the dome proved overly saturated as well.

Another disappointment for Belluschi was the design of the bema. Envisioning it as the opportunity for a major artistic masterpiece and the dramatic focal point of the interior, he had hoped to bring in a well-known abstract artist such as Adolph Gottlieb or Theodore Roszak, as he had done with the Portsmouth Abbey (no. 13).

Belluschi recommended Sasaki, Walker and Associates for the landscaping, who gave the surroundings a Japanese sensibility and simplicity fully consistent with Belluschi's clear structural form.

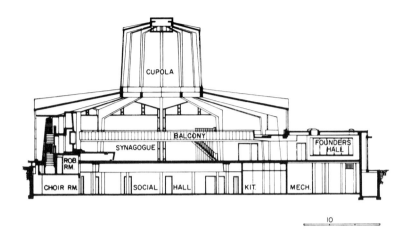

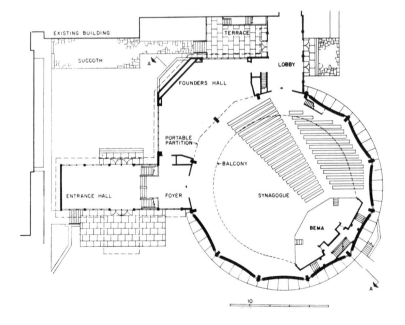

REFERENCES

Belluschi, Pietro. "Notes by the Architects on the Design of Temple Adath Israel in Merion, Pennsylvania." Manuscript, George Arents Research Library, Syracuse University.

"Building Types Study No. 272: Pietro Belluschi, Synagogue for Temple Adath Israel." *Architectural Record* 126, no. 1 (July 1959): 154–59.

16. CEDAR LANE UNITARIAN CHURCH

Small Unitarian church in Bethesda, Maryland (1955–58)
Architect: Pietro Belluschi; associates: Keyes, Lethbridge & Condon

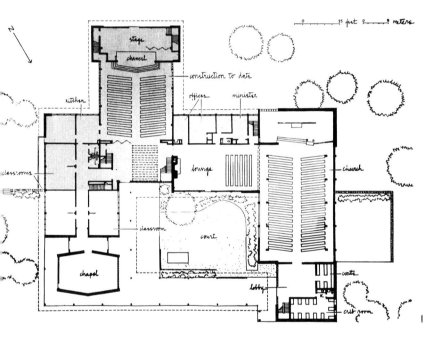

The overall program for this Unitarian church called for several buildings to be erected over time, beginning with a 250-seat assembly hall, then classrooms and a children's chapel, and finally the main church, which was never built. The assembly hall, the only part for which Belluschi was responsible, was to serve as a church until the rest of the complex was finished; it was completed in 1958.

The site was originally deeply wooded, providing inspiration for Belluschi's scheme. To his dismay, most of the trees were removed for parking during the course of construction, substantially changing the character of the building he had initially envisioned.

The structure is of reinforced concrete and steel in conformity with local building code requirements, with wood siding on the exterior to harmonize with the natural setting. The roof is of cedar shingles, and retaining walls are of a local red-brown sandstone.

REFERENCES

"Four Houses of Worship (Unitarian Church, Bethesda, Maryland)." *Progressive Architecture* 40, no. 6 (June 1959): 118–21.

17. CHURCH OF THE REDEEMER

Large church for an Episcopalian congregation in Baltimore, Maryland (1954–58)
Architect: Pietro Belluschi; associates: Rogers, Taliaferro & Lamb
Cost: $950,000

The Episcopalian Church of the Redeemer, the result of a highly rewarding, openly collaborative design process like that of Cottage Grove Presbyterian of a decade earlier (no. 11), proved to be one of Belluschi's finest churches. It was also one of the most challenging. The program called for a new sanctuary to be added to an existing hundred-year-old church on a beautifully wooded, spacious, 9-acre lot bounded on all sides by streets in an affluent, growing neighborhood at the outskirts of Baltimore. The principal design problem consisted of relating the new, substantially larger, one-thousand-seat structure to the existing small stone 1858 English Parish church without overwhelming it in size or stature. A second objective was to fit a large number of subsidiary buildings—administration building, parish house, fellowship hall, and Sunday school—unobtrusively into the site, so as not to mar its natural beauty. These considerations were found to be minor, however, in light of what proved to be the most taxing problem of all: convincing the conservative congregation of the appropriateness of a modern design.

As Belluschi was then very busy, living in Boston and dividing his time among the deanship at MIT, his numerous other professional obligations, and the demands of his family, he relied heavily on his associates Rogers, Taliaferro & Lamb. Francis Taliaferro had long admired Belluschi's work—its discretion, respect for natural materials, fine craftsmanship—in short, its sensitivity to the legacy of Frank Lloyd Wright and the Arts and Crafts movement, which represented, to him, modernism at its finest. Drawing on current technology, Belluschi adhered to the principles of modernism while avoiding trendy formalism. Sympathetic to these aims, Taliaferro and his associates felt privileged to work with Belluschi; Belluschi in turn respected them. This mutual

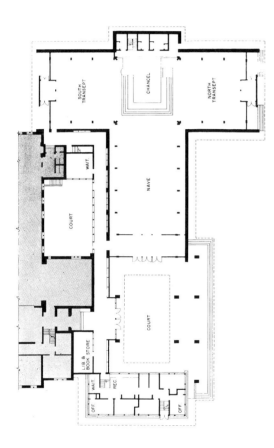

respect and spirit of genuine teamwork, representing brainstorming at its best, led in large measure to the success of the Baltimore church.

Their first challenge was to work out a suitable site plan. Belluschi had originally thought of siting the new church to the south of the old, between it and a side street. His associates suggested instead demolishing an existing refectory on the north side of the old church, incorporating its stone in the new construction to ensure continuity, and locating the new sanctuary there. This freed up the southern portion of the lot and enabled them to cluster the buildings in the middle, surrounding them on all sides by spacious landscaping. The buildings were grouped in a tightly knit, interlocking grid of cruciform, L-, and U-shaped buildings, all interconnected by covered loggias and forming a series of private, inner, landscaped courtyards.

The new sanctuary was to be linked to the original church, henceforth to be used as a chapel, by an existing fellowship hall and parish house, with an open, landscaped garden between. The orientation of the new church was reversed to avoid having a competing entrance on the principal street front. The new entrance thus faces east rather than west, allowing easy access to the parking lot in back. In a progression of spaces typical of Belluschi, the entrance opens off an enclosed, landscaped court, which the visitor enters through a spacious loggia.

Representing a highly successful integration of different design idioms, the new Church of the Redeemer is distinctly modern yet meshes harmoniously with the old. Drawing on the historicized English Parish church in its overall massing, pitch of the gabled roofs, materials of stone, wood, and slate, and cruciform plan, the new church is nonetheless clearly nontraditional. At the request of the congregation, it has no spire, so that the steeple of the old church remains the visual climax of the complex.

The structural system of the new church consists of a freestanding internal framework of laminated, pointed arches that carry the roof. Spanning the nave and the transepts, they intersect over the crossing, providing a visual focal point throughout the sanctuary for the altar below. In profile they repeat the purely decorative ribs of the plaster vault of the Gothic Revival church, linking the old and new visually and symbolically but also drawing a clear analogy between the struc-

tural rationalism of the modern structure and that of the true Gothic nave. This consistent logic is carried out on the exterior by the bearing, laminated arches of the gables with their crow's-nest extensions, echoing the decorative stickwork of the original 1858 church. Nonloadbearing exterior walls use stone from the demolished refectory and from the same quarry as the original church. They are low, so that in profile the roof dominates. Above them runs a narrow, continuous window band of wood screening and colored glass, underscoring the walls' purely screening rather than loadbearing function.

To accommodate the requisite number of seats, a cross-axial plan like that of the original church was used but now with generous transepts almost equal in width to the nave. Rather than housed in a traditional isolating chancel, the altar was brought forward into the crossing and placed on a raised platform, consistent with current thinking on liturgical reform and the Reverend Bennett Sims's request for a communal rather than hierarchical plan. As is customary in the Episcopalian service, which gives equal emphasis to the sacrament, preaching, and reading of the Scriptures, the altar is in the center, with pulpit and lectern to either side. The choir and organ are located in the northern transept; the sacristy is behind the chancel, concealed from view by a monumental stained-glass screen.

The nave is dim, enshrouded by the great, hovering roof of dark-stained wood, lit only by the narrow zone of variegated colored glass—deep blue, jade, ruby—which runs continuously around the nave at the base of the roof, tying the whole together in a simple jeweled band. This narrow zone of light, like that between the canted wall and sweeping roof of Le Corbusier's Ronchamp Chapel, effectively isolates the roof so that it hovers, seemingly suspended, above the sanctuary. The band of vivid, saturated colored light is complemented by the paler, screened amber tones of the high gable windows of the transepts. Extending beyond the summit of the soaring arches and supported on crow's-nest trusses, the ridgepole of the roof fades into darkness, creating a "mysterious attic" that lends further drama to the nave.

The focal point of the nave and complex as a whole is a brilliant stained-glass window, a monumental altar screen filling the arch of the chancel wall. Designed by the renowned artist Gyorgy Kepes, a colleague of Belluschi at MIT, it consists of randomly shaped pieces of

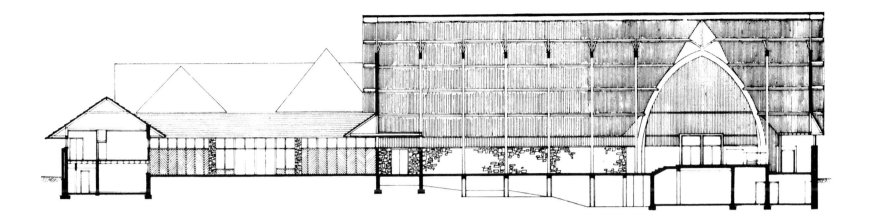

colored glass held in a fragile filigree of concrete and epoxy. Produced in the workshops of Gabriel Loire in Chartres, France, the window was one of the first uses in the United States of the modern stained- (or more accurately, colored) glass technique. Skillfully grading the proportion of glass to mortar from bottom to top, with thicker mortar at the base thinning to the merest of slender lines above, and varying the hues of the glass so that it changes from heavily saturated color to virtual white, Kepes created a luminous, implicit image of the cross. Serving as a foil for the highly polished, pure white marble altar, the window functions as a magnificent dramatic climax to Belluschi's carefully orchestrated progression of spaces.

A slender metal cross by the sculptor Ronald Hayes Pearson, suspended over the altar, complements the Kepes glass. Etched to the point of skeletal frailty, it is barely visible, coming into one's consciousness only gradually as one grows accustomed to the dim light. Other furnishings—pulpit, lectern, altar rail, and candlesticks—were all designed by the architects or artists under their direction.

Though initially excited by having a man of Belluschi's caliber as their architect, the congregation resisted his proposal. Shocked by his initial presentation, many church members found his work repellent and remained steadfastly opposed to a modern design. After several years of reworking, a revised scheme was put to a vote. It was approved, but not overwhelmingly, and only because of the unflagging support of the by-then convinced, enthusiastic young pastor, the Reverend Bennett Sims.

Belluschi was known for his humanistic interpretation of modernism. An incident at the Church of the Redeemer bears this out. Belluschi insisted that the stone walls of the new church be deliberately rustic rather than smooth and refined, with irregular, rough-hewn fieldstone and an even thicker, more textured mortar than was used in the original nineteenth-century church. On the one hand, this desire reflected the current interest among architects in the imperfect forms of vernacular architecture, a counterpart to the sleek, machine-polished, refined forms of the Miesian ideal. But the decision also bore evidence of Belluschi's awareness of the people involved, the masons and their handiwork. Such handwrought surfaces would serve, he argued, as testimony of an earlier time when fine craftsmanship was valued and would be a useful reminder to the current generation that churches were once built by men, not machines.

Ostensibly in keeping with the 1858 English Parish church, the Church of the Redeemer is in fact more Japanese—from the great, hovering, pyramidal roof with its *irimoye* profile and elegant wood craftsmanship, to the secluded Japanese landscaped gardens and their spirit of Zen. A heightened interest in Japanese architecture was sweeping the country at the time as a result of a major exhibition at the Museum of Modern Art, New York, in 1954–55. Belluschi visited Japan for the first time, in June 1956, while the design of the Church of the Redeemer was in progress. His scheme for the church pays homage to this design tradition, which he himself had long revered. Also reflected in the design is his exposure to contemporary theology and the writings

of Alfred North Whitehead and Paul Tillich, whose work he found to be of greater significance than that of the architectural theorists.

The Church of the Redeemer was a demanding project, one Belluschi could not have done without the support of all those involved and their full commitment to his architectural ideals—his associates, the pastor, the landscape architect, and the artists. The whole ensemble, from site planning and design to landscaping and interior finishes, was governed by a single overriding aesthetic. Based on his conception of modern architecture, with its legacy of structural rationalism, Frank Lloyd Wright, and Arts and Crafts ideals, informed by Japanese as well as vernacular architecture, and given depth by his understanding of traditional and contemporary religious values, the Church of the Redeemer stands as a personal expression of what Belluschi envisioned the church in the modern world could be. It proved to be one of Belluschi's most successful churches, with its reticent, unpretentious, yet thoroughly modern forms harmonizing with both the old church and the natural environment; its progression of spaces from the secular world of streets and parking lots through a quiet, landscaped garden into a spiritually compelling, uplifting space; and its creation of a space both warm and intimate, comforting and familiar, yet lofty and inspirational. The explicit, consistent rationality of its structural system bespeaks the clarity of human thought; the vast, mysterious space and inspiring brilliant light from the rich stained glass evoke the mystery of God and the unknowns of an infinite universe. The Church of the Redeemer represents Belluschi's ideals of church design at their finest—rational structure, appropriate scale, harmonious proportions, exquisite materials and fine craftsmanship, subdued but dramatic lighting, and an eloquent, moving space.

In 1960 the Church of the Redeemer received a national award of merit from the American Institute of Architects, and in 1986 a twenty-five-year award from the Baltimore chapter of the institute.

REFERENCES

"Building Types Study No. 272: Pietro Belluschi, Church of the Redeemer." *Architectural Record* 126, no. 1 (July 1959): cover and 164–70.

"Award of Merit, Pietro Belluschi; Rogers, Taliaferro and Lamb, Associated Architects." *Journal of the American Institute of Architects* 33, no. 4 (Apr. 1960): 89.

Time Magazine, Dec. 26, 1960, 28–32.

Von Eckhardt, Wolf, ed. *Mid-Century Architecture in America. Honor Awards of the American Institute of Architects, 1949–1961* (Baltimore: Johns Hopkins Press, 1961), p. 144.

Christ-Janer, Albert, and Mary Mix Foley. *Modern Church Architecture: A Guide to the Form and Spirit of Twentieth-Century Religious Buildings* (New York: McGraw-Hill, 1962), pp. 171–83.

Taped interviews: Gyorgy Kepes with author, Mar. 29, 1989; Francis Taliaferro and Archibald Rogers with author, Apr. 17, 1989.

Clausen, Meredith L. "Transparent Structure: Belluschi Churches of the 1950s." *Faith and Form* 24 (Fall 1990): 10–14.

18. TRINITY EPISCOPAL CHURCH

Mid-sized Episcopal church in Concord, Massachusetts (1959–63)
Architect: Pietro Belluschi; associated architects: Anderson, Beckwith & Haible
Cost estimate in 1960: $689,000

A sophisticated but conservative congregation in the growing, affluent community of Concord needed a larger sanctuary but did not want to give up its small parish church, which fit the character of the traditional New England town. The problem was thus to add an enlarged church that would seat four hundred on a relatively cramped lot without affecting the character of the existing church, which would thenceforth be used as a chapel. The budget was adequate but not substantial. The site was in a wooded, semirural residential neighborhood twenty minutes west of Boston.

Belluschi presented the congregation with two alternative schemes, one with a conventional, longitudinal nave and simple gabled roof, the other more modern, with a centralized, octagonal plan and folded pyramidal roof. His proposals provoked further discussion, with the result that the lot was expanded and the site changed to the other side of the existing church to allow more room for an education unit as well as a new sanctuary.

Aware of the cool reception his modern scheme had initially received, Belluschi with a revised program returned to a traditional, longitudinal plan. He used as his point of departure the form of Zion Lutheran in Portland (no. 8), with its gabled roof terminating in a colonnaded hipped roof to form the narthex and portico. In the Concord scheme, the proportions differed: the roof dominated, and its pitch was steeper, suggesting the influence of Gunnar Asplund's Woodland Chapel (see fig. 12) or, more likely, a Japanese inspiration (see fig. 13). Belluschi's scheme echoed the pitch of the original gabled church and used the same local fieldstone for the exterior walls to sustain continuity between the old and new buildings.

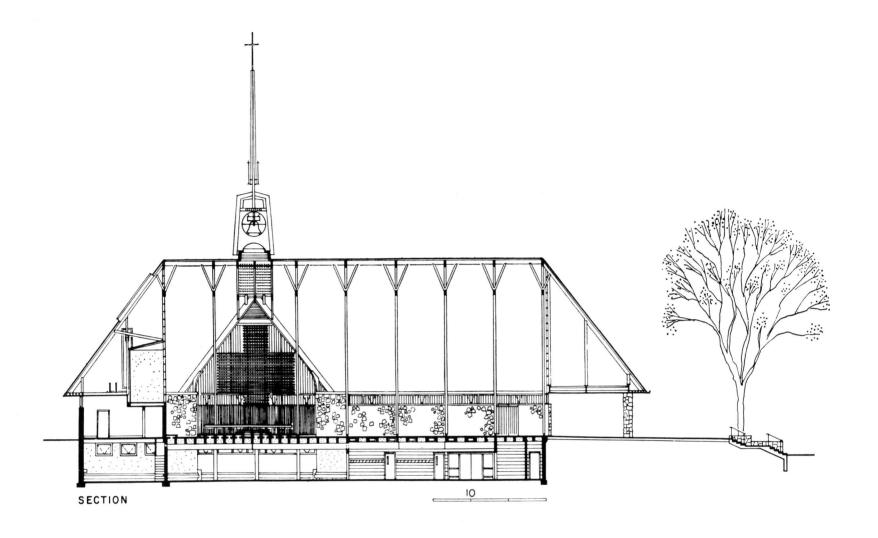

SECTION

10

The plan consists of a simple rectangular nave with short transepts forming a cross-axis. As in the Church of the Redeemer (no. 17), the chancel is pulled into the crossing and raised several steps for visual and symbolic prominence. Based on a concept of a freestanding, exposed wooden framework enclosed by non-loadbearing walls, Concord Trinity drew on a rich heritage of Belluschi churches: the Church of the Redeemer, Zion Lutheran, and the still earlier St. Thomas More (no. 3). The sanctuary is vaulted by an exposed wooden roof supported on a series of simple, freestanding, laminated, pointed arches, with low, non-loadbearing enclosure walls of randomly laid fieldstone. A thin zone of tinted glass, as in the Church of the Redeemer, forms a continuous clerestory just under the eaves and provides the main source of light in the nave. Shedding brilliant natural light on the altar is a raised cupola, or lantern, which, like that of St. Thomas More, was to have been crowned on the exterior by a tall, slender spire.

The focal point of the nave is the monumental window in the chancel end, behind the altar. As in the Church of the Redeemer, this is a Gyorgy Kepes design, here with a simple triangle symbolizing the Trinity as the only imagery. Unlike the Church of the Redeemer window, which is lit artificially from behind, natural light comes from a skylight in the roof over the sacristy behind the chancel. Rather than filling the apsidal end, the Kepes window takes up only the upper portion of the wall; below, a wooden grille conceals organ pipes that form a backdrop for the altar.

The solution was simple, inspired as much by Tillich's philosophy of holy emptiness as by circumstances of sight and program. In Belluschi's words, the final plan was "a statement of the importance of humility and of emphasizing the qualities of space over the pretensions of form."

Pews designed by Belluschi were assembled and finished by the parishioners themselves. And, as at the Church of the Redeemer, Belluschi urged the Concord Episcopal congregation to leave the masons' strike marks on the stones of the nave walls, in recognition of their work and a sign of the collectivity of the endeavor.

REFERENCES

"Building Types Study No. 272: Pietro Belluschi, Trinity Episcopal Church Scheme No. 1 and Scheme No. 2." *Architectural Record* 126, no. 1 (July 1959): 160–63.

"Addition to a Small Gothic Church." *Architectural Record* 129, no. 7 (June 1961): 122–25.

"Episcopal Church by Belluschi." *Architectural Record* 135, no. 3 (Mar. 1964): 145–48.

Hayes, Bartlett. *Tradition Becomes Innovation: Modern Religious Architecture in America* (New York: Pilgrim Press, 1983), pp. 91, 147.

Taped interviews: Gyorgy Kepes with author, Mar. 29, 1989 (A renowned artist in his own right, Kepes was an MIT colleague who collaborated with Belluschi on a number of church projects); Frederic L. Day, Jr., with author, Mar. 31, 1989 (Day was an architect with Carl Koch and Associates who later worked with Belluschi on the Park Avenue Congregational Church [no. 19] and a member of the Trinity Episcopal congregation); Lawrence B. Anderson with author, Apr. 2, 1989 (Anderson was chair of the architecture department at MIT when Belluschi was dean and served as associate with Belluschi on the Concord and Portsmouth Abbey projects).

19. PARK AVENUE CONGREGATIONAL CHURCH

Small suburban church in Arlington, Massachusetts (1959–61)
Architect: Pietro Belluschi; associates: Carl Koch & Associates;
project architect: Frederic L. Day, Jr.
Cost: $193,000

With the commission for a new Congregational church in the town of Arlington outside Boston, Belluschi faced a seemingly impossible challenge: the addition of a new sanctuary between an existing parish hall and former church school building, on a tightly constricted, roughly triangular lot bordered by streets on both sides. The budget was equally restrictive. A third major factor was the need to relate the new building to the white-trimmed, brick Georgian Parish house on one side and the wood-frame building on the other.

Proving his skill at efficient planning and contextual design, and at obtaining maximum effect with a minimum of means, Belluschi came up with a simple brick and concrete building with a remarkably spacious interior, longitudinal in plan and vaulted by a low, pitched roof borne on laminated bents.

One enters directly off the street into a small, angled narthex that faces a quiet, secluded garden and opens at right angles onto the rectangular nave running roughly parallel to the street. Pews are angled to save space and to maximize sight lines of the communion table. The chancel end is also angled for design continuity.

On the interior, an exposed roof of fir finished only with a preservative is supported on a series of low, broad, pointed, laminated Douglas fir arches. These split as they rise to meet overhead in the center of each bay, analogous to Gothic rib vaulting. Free of a load-bearing function, the exterior walls are of finely detailed brick and are without ornamentation other than regular breaks in the coursing of the masonry that articulate the modules of the structural system; thus they serve principally as screens to shut out noise and distractions from the street.

The interior is lit by a continuous clerestory zone on the street side of the nave only. Focus on the chancel is provided by the lighting, with a floor-to-ceiling window-wall of stained glass on the east side.

Using humble means and no ornamentation, Belluschi sought a distinctive architecture as he had in the Church of St. Thomas More (no. 3), simply by the skillful contrast of varying textures, hues, and grains of common materials: natural woods, exposed brick, and stained glass. The only color other than the glass is that of a warm plum carpet.

The only traditional symbols are the tall, slender spire that surmounts a polygonal cupola marking the chancel, and a simple brass cross suspended over the altar.

REFERENCES

"Church Designed for Difficult Site and Low Budget." *Architectural Record* 130 (Nov. 1961): 143–48.

Taped interview, Frederic L. Day, Jr., with author, Mar. 31, 1989.

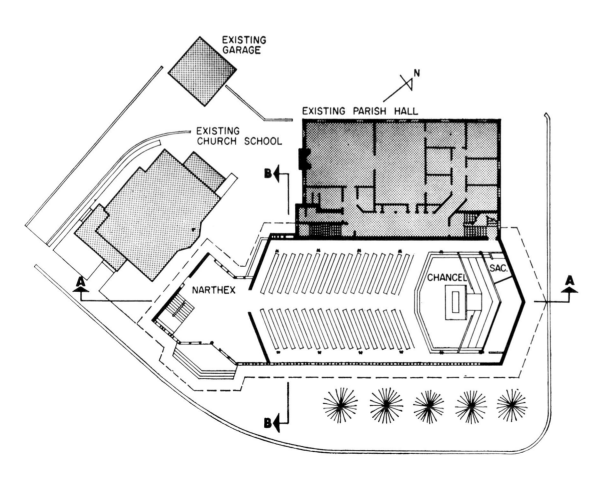

EXISTING
GARAGE

EXISTING
CHURCH SCHOOL

N

EXISTING PARISH HALL

B

NARTHEX

A   A

CHANCEL   SAC.

B

20. TEMPLE B'RITH KODESH

Large synagogue in Rochester, New York (1959–63)
Architect: Pietro Belluschi; associates: Waasdorp, Northrup & Austin;
project architect: Marvin M. Meyer
Cost: $2.5 million

In 1959, Belluschi was asked by the Temple B'rith Kodesh to design a large complex of religious and educational buildings on a spacious, flat, 15-acre landscaped site in an affluent residential neighborhood of Rochester, New York. The sanctuary, seating a congregation of 1,250, was to dominate as both a symbol of the synagogue and a visual landmark.

His solution consisted of a monumental 65-foot-high, twelve-sided dome rising above a cluster of simple one- and two-story buildings housing educational and other subsidiary facilities. The entrance to the complex is through a broad loggia leading into a quiet, landscaped courtyard, with the sanctuary to one side and classrooms to the other, and a small, lozenge-shaped chapel for private functions at the far end.

The synagogue has a steel-frame structure, with low, peripheral walls of warm, rosy brick, above which rises the dome; its sides are glazed, screened by panels of stained redwood. Flashing and downspouts are of black copper.

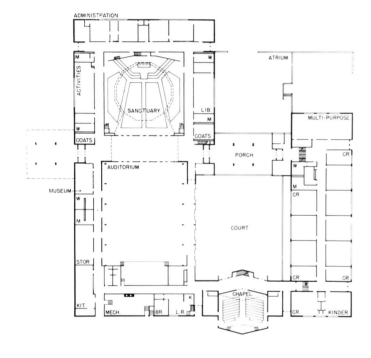

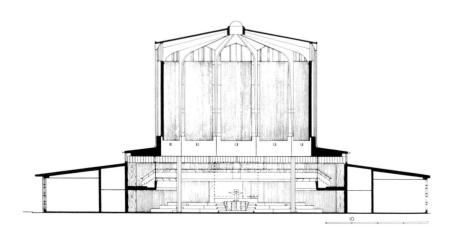

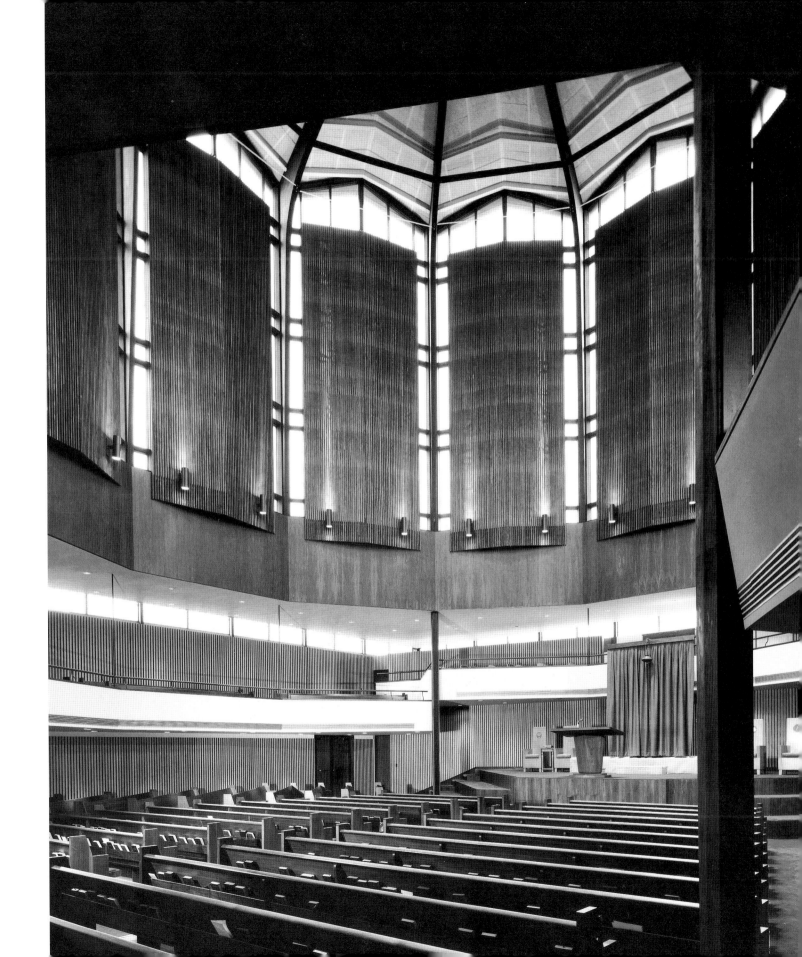

Conceived during the summer Belluschi spent in Rome, the sanctuary is vaulted by a tall framed structure of steel bents, which meet overhead in an oculus like that of the Pantheon. The glazing between the structural ribs is screened by narrow, convex panels of sound-absorbing redwood, one per bay, so that the sanctuary reads as a light-weight, screened structure symbolizing the traditional Judaic tent. The walls of the sanctuary below are of maple, with contrasting battens of walnut. Pews are also of walnut.

The focal point of the sanctuary is a sculpted bronze ark by the New York artist Luise Kaish. A smaller ark of welded metal by Richard Filipowski, a colleague of Belluschi and a professor of design at MIT, provides the centerpiece of the private chapel.

Noted for its promise of a smoothly functioning plan and its clear expression of religious purpose, the Rochester temple received an award of merit from the New York chapter of the American Institute of Architects while still in the project stage.

REFERENCES

"Church Designed for Difficult Site and Low Budget." *Architectural Record* 130, no. 5 (Nov. 1961): 143–48.

"A Major Synagogue by Belluschi." *Architectural Record* 134 (Nov. 1963): 143–48.

Recent American Synagogue Architecture. Exh. cat. (New York: Jewish Museum, 1963), pp. 19, 26–27.

21. TRINITY CHURCH ADDITION

Project for an addition of a small chapel to Henry Hobson Richardson's Trinity Church, Copley Square, Boston, Massachusetts (1960)
Architect: Pietro Belluschi; assistant: Robert Brannen; associates: Shepley, Bulfinch, Richardson & Abbott
Estimated cost: $601,200

The commission was disarmingly simple: to add a small chapel to Henry Hobson Richardson's Episcopalian Trinity Church, on the corner of St. James Avenue and Clarendon in Boston. The 120-seat chapel was to provide quarters for the Sunday school, a place for private devotional services, and an intimate sanctuary for small weddings, funerals, baptisms, and other small group services. The site was cramped, and the integrity of the existing structure had to be preserved on all sides. The biggest challenge was the design: how to add a fully modern chapel to one of the nation's most revered historic buildings.

Belluschi's proposal called for a chapel of a scale and identity all its own. Oval in plan and utterly simple in form, it was to have been, like Mies's chapel at the Illinois Institute of Technology in Chicago (see fig. 26) and Eero Saarinen's at MIT, exquisite in execution, a tiny jewel. The design involved the collaboration of two major artists, Gyorgy Kepes for the stained glass incorporated into the wall, and the Italian sculptor Mirko Basaldella for an ornamental metal sculpture at the entrance. As simple in design as Richardson's was complex, the chapel was meant to be sympathetic to the existing historic building in materials, form, pitch of roof, color, and texture, yet unequivocally of its own time.

The project did not proceed, evidently because of cost.

REFERENCES

"An Addition to a Masterpiece." *Architectural Record* 129, no. 7 (June 1961): 126–27.

Taped interview, Jean Paul Carlhian with author, Mar. 29, 1989 (Carlhian was an architect in the Shepley, Bulfinch, Richardson & Abbott office about the time of the Trinity Church addition).

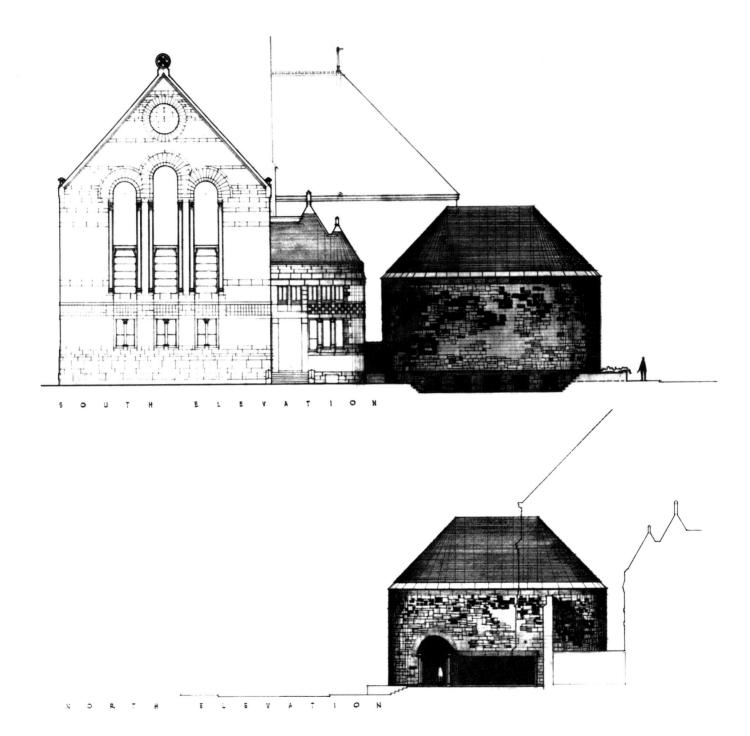

S O U T H   E L E V A T I O N

N O R T H   E L E V A T I O N

22. MAY MEMORIAL UNITARIAN SOCIETY

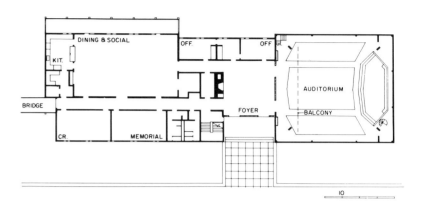

Simple, low-cost church for a Unitarian congregation in Syracuse, New York (1961–65)

Architect: Pietro Belluschi; associates: Pederson Hueber Hares & Glavin; assistant: Robert Brannen

Cost: $373,000

After rejecting a proposal from Paul Rudolph considered too assertive, the democratically minded Unitarian congregation of the May Memorial Society in Syracuse wanted nothing more than a simple, quiet, functional place for communal worship, modern but unpretentious. The budget was limited; hence a compact, economical plan was paramount. Equally important was the concern that there be no religious symbolism.

In its absence of explicit religious imagery, Belluschi's scheme draws on the legacy of New England meetinghouses, from the four-square Old Ship Meeting House of 1681 in Hingham, Massachusetts (see fig. 48), to Frank Lloyd Wright's Unity Temple of 1906 in Oak Park, Illinois, but now recast in terms of the 1960s and imbued with a distinctly Japanese sensibility. On a narrow, wooded site on the outskirts of the city, bordered on the front by a major street and sloping steeply to a stream in the back, Belluschi laid out the three functional units of the complex laterally, with the auditorium to one side, social-meeting hall on the other, and a foyer between. Classrooms are on a lower level overlooking the stream. The form is kept low, with the second story pressed into the hillside and visible only from the rear.

A low pyramidal roof with raised lantern over the sanctuary distinguishes it from the other two wings, which have simple pitched roofs. The interior of the sanctuary is realized in different woods with contrasting grains and hues. Four great freestanding laminated fir arches rise from the corners of the nearly square plan, meeting in the centralized square oculus, or lantern, overhead. The walls are of solid roof decking, with cedar wood siding on the exterior, and at the rear of the sanctuary is a choir loft and organ—all familiar Belluschi elements, but now handled in a new way.

Consistent with the congregation's request for no religious symbolism, Belluschi designed the auditorium space without a central focus. A grooved screen serves as a backdrop for the speaker's platform; a simple, low shelf holds arrangements of flowers, plants, candelabra, or other appropriate objects. Stained glass is confined to the foyer and sanctuary and consists of a screen cast in abstract patterns of muted tones held in place by slender wood mullions.

The only decorative element in the sanctuary, members of the congregation like to say, is the fortuitous flickering image of a butterfly cast on the wall behind the speaker's platform, created when sunlight filtering through the squared oculus hits at just the right angle—a serendipitous happening fully in the Zen spirit.

REFERENCES

"A Unitarian Church by Belluschi." *Architectural Record* 138, no. 6 (Dec. 1965): 118–20.

Interviews: David Ashley (architect and member of the congregation) with author; Douglas Aird (engineer and member of the congregation) with author; Robert Coye, Frances E. Hares, and J. Murray Hueber (Hueber, Hares, Glavin) with author, Oct. 25–26, 1986.

23. FIRST COMMUNITY CHURCH

Project for a large, centralized church for a nondenominational congregation affiliated with the United Church of Christ, Columbus, Ohio (1961)
Architect: Pietro Belluschi; associates: Brubaker/Brandt; assistant: Robert Brannen
Projected budget: $3 million

The job consisted of a large church for a well-to-do, six-thousand-member congregation representing many of the most prominent families of the community. The site, on 22.5 acres of flat, unwooded land, allowed complete freedom in design and landscaping. The projected budget was substantial.

For this project, Belluschi, working with the young designers in the Cambridge office of Eduardo Catalano, developed a number of highly sculptural schemes bearing the influence of the newer, Corbusier-inspired, Brutalist trends in architecture. Most of the schemes were centralized in plan, with imposing polygonal domes supported on an internal framework of exposed, laminated wooden bents. Lighting was to come from above, either by monitor windows that washed walls with a soft light, or by skylights, or a combination of both. The exteriors were to have been of granite or brick.

Although intended to be one of the major church buildings in the area, the First Community Church was not built, as insufficient funds were available.

REFERENCES
Taped interview, Robert Brannen with author, Apr. 6, 1989 (Brannen was Belluschi's assistant working in the Catalano office at the time).
Letter, Leland Brubaker to author, Dec. 1990–Jan. 1991.

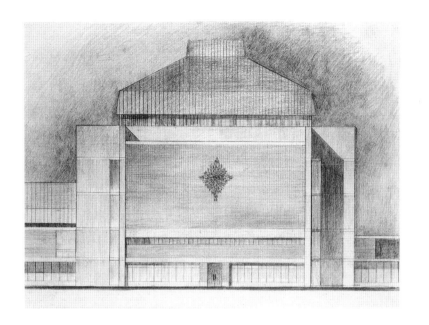

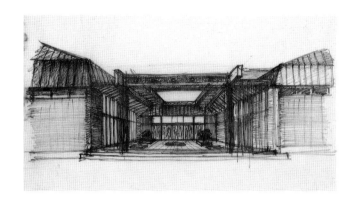

24. FIRST METHODIST CHURCH

Large urban church in Duluth, Minnesota (1962–71)
Architect: Pietro Belluschi; assistant: Robert Brannen; associates: Melander, Fugelso & Associates

In this commission, which closely followed the First Community Church (no. 23) in Columbus, Belluschi sought a form that would be "strongly symbolic and visible from a great distance," a simple, bold, sculptural form that would exert a monumental presence on its spacious site at the top of the hill. In so doing, he pursued the direction of early 1960s Brutalist architecture, which leaned toward the design of large, compelling images.

The design also bore the influence of the theologian Paul Tillich. As traditional symbolism lost its meaning in the modern world, one of the few remaining viable symbols of the church was—or should be, Tillich argued—the church building itself. Tillich was also in the

thoughts of the congregation's pastor, who wrote to Belluschi of the theologian's concept of holy emptiness, hoping the Duluth church would achieve the same "majestic simplicity" he had found in the interiors of Zion Lutheran in Portland (no. 8) and the Church of the Redeemer in Baltimore (no. 17).

At one point Belluschi regarded First Methodist as the most important church of his career. Thinking on a far larger scale than he ever had before, and working with a substantial budget of roughly $1 million, he sought a design whose cross plan would symbolize the togetherness of congregation and clergy and whose form would express the strength, simplicity, and structural integrity of the Gothic tradition. Seeking a structural system that would provide both a monumental image and the requisite amount of sanctuary space, he confronted the same problem he was to face in St. Mary's Cathedral in San Francisco (no. 26): balancing the proportions of a broad square base and lofty vault without losing the intimacy of a sacred space. The solution, worked out with the help of several designers in Eduardo Catalano's office, was to mount a steeply sloped pyramidal dome over a broad 60-foot-square base. Rigorously symmetrical, imposing in scale, and unfenestrated except for the series of triangular skylights at the base of the dome, with exteriors of light pink granite and a roof of copper shingle, the church marked a new direction in Belluschi's work.

REFERENCES

Letters: Belluschi to Rev. E. J. Walker; Belluschi to A. Reinhold Melander, Nov.–Dec. 1962 (Belluschi Collection, George Arents Research Library, Syracuse University).

Tillich, Paul. "On the Theology of Fine Art and Architecture" [1961], in *On Art and Architecture*, ed. John Dillenberger and Jane Dillenberger (New York: Crossroad Publishing, 1987), pp. 204–13.

25. CHURCH OF THE CHRISTIAN UNION

Large Unitarian church in Rockford, Illinois (1962–66)
Architect: Pietro Belluschi; associates: C. Edward Ware Associates;
assistant: Robert Brannen

The Rockford Unitarian church, although like the May Memorial (no. 22) in its free-spirited, nontraditional approach, was wholly unlike it in form. Belluschi felt that the site, a spacious 10.5 acres on a slope of bare, rolling hills in east Rockford, called for a compelling statement:

> It needed a strong symbolic expression, a form removed from the old uninspired ecclesiastical tradition, yet possessing convincing qualities particularly relevant to the Unitarian commitments. To this end, we endeavored to give the building structural integrity and to fulfill the program given to us with maximum economy, yet without cheapness. We strove to give clarity to the plan, while providing a sequence of visual experiences, relying on good proportions, effective lighting, and honest materials.

Suggesting current trends in Brutalist architecture and the pervasive influence of Le Corbusier and Louis Kahn, the Church of the Christian Union was given a bold, geometric form of a new sculptural complexity. Different functional spaces were broken into component parts,

B

OFF. OFF.

A — — A

LOUNGE

ATRIUM

NARTHEX

K.

MULTI-PURPOSE

B

UPPER LEVEL

10

the forms themselves broken up, and the parts staggered to conform to the slope of the site. The sanctuary, clearly articulated by its height, was to one side of the narthex, which formed a link between it and the fellowship hall, offices, library, lounge, and small kitchen on the other side. Classrooms and a small chapel were located in a story below.

Characteristically, the rationalized structural system is expressed on the interior. A series of powerful, elemental, H-shaped, monolithic supports of precast concrete bears the flat roof; these also define the repeated bays of the nave, as in a traditional church. Vertical board-and-batten panels of stained redwood between the exposed concrete supports soften visually and acoustically the effect of hard, flat surfaces.

The nave is lit by warmly colored glass embedded in the vertical members of the concrete supports, the illumination supplemented by a continuous clerestory along the crest of the nave wall. The chancel is lit by Belluschi's familiar full-length window-wall of stained glass in an abstracted wooden grille.

A bare branch that a member of the congregation brought from a nearby field just before the dedication provided an element of the natural—a Zen touch characteristic of the 1960s.

REFERENCES

"Tradition-free Architecture for a 'Free Church': A Unitarian Center." *Architectural Record* 141, no. 3 (Mar. 1967): 135–40.

Interview, Alan G. Deale with author, 1989 (Deale was minister of the Rockford church at the time it was built).

26. ST. MARY'S CATHEDRAL

Roman Catholic cathedral in San Francisco, California (1963–70)
Design architect: Pietro Belluschi; assistant: Robert Brannen; engineering consultant: Pier Luigi Nervi; associates: McSweeney, Ryan & Lee; structural engineers: Leonard F. Robinson & Associates; geotechnical consultants: Woodward-Lundgren & Associates, Oakland
Cost: $8.5 million

St. Mary's Cathedral offered Belluschi a rare architectural experience: the design of a major twentieth-century cathedral for the city of San Francisco. It also presented the challenge Mies van der Rohe in 1960 had said would be impossible to meet: "This is not a great cathedral-building age, like the Middle Ages. Today, if you tried to build a cathedral, you would succeed only in building a big church. Not religion but technology is the controlling spirit of the age."

In September 1962 a fire destroyed the old St. Mary's Cathedral in San Francisco. The following January, Belluschi received a letter from the architect John Carl Warnecke telling him of plans to rebuild the cathedral. A team of local architects chosen by Archbishop Joseph T. McGucken had already begun work on the project, but in light of the momentousness of the commission, many architects, donors, and the public in general questioned the propriety of the selection. Warnecke wondered if Belluschi, as dean at MIT and one of the most prominent names in contemporary church architecture, might be interested. Belluschi responded immediately: "No architect in his right mind would refuse to be considered for such a job." Although he heard little more about it and nothing formal until early summer, Belluschi immediately began to think of possible design solutions.

It was a daunting proposition. Belluschi had to devise a new form completely of its time yet expressive of its sacred purpose. Le Corbusier's chapel at Ronchamp (see fig. 24) in the 1950s had broken thoroughly with historical form and opened the way to a new sculptural

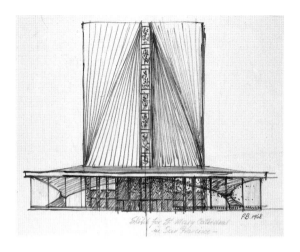

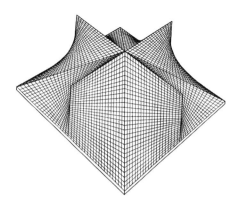

Eduardo Catalano. *Structures of Warped Surfaces*. The Student Publication of the School of Design, vol. 10, no. 1 (Raleigh, N.C., 1960).

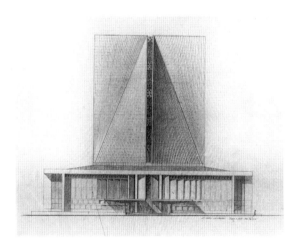

direction in church design. Other architects, too, such as Felix Candela, Eduardo Torroja, Pier Luigi Nervi, and Kenzo Tange, were exploring church design using structurally expressive, thin-shell structures. MIT had by the mid-1950s become one of the leading centers of experimentation in concrete shell structures. By this time, Belluschi was working in association with the Argentinian architect Eduardo Catalano, whom he had brought to MIT as an instructor and who had become one of his closest friends; through him, Belluschi had become interested in the potential of warped surfaces in thin shell concrete. Other precedents were Nervi's project for a cathedral in New Norcia, Australia, with its three 100-foot-high paraboloid vaults on a broad triangular base 240 feet long on each side, and Tange's new St. Mary's Cathedral in Tokyo (see fig. 44)—cruciform in plan, with eight hyperbolic paraboloids joined at the top and sides with vertical windows of stained glass, the entire structure poised on a plain, broad podium.

Drawing on these current developments and using a study from Catalano's recently published book, *Structures of Warped Surfaces*, as his point of departure, Belluschi envisioned a great hovering shell of reinforced concrete hyperbolic paraboloids rising in quadrants out of a square plan, joined on each side and at the summit by narrow panels of stained glass to form a great cross. All forces of the huge vault were to be funneled onto four great sculptural pylons, themselves formed of hyperbolic paraboloids, one at each corner of the plan. This would create a centralized sanctuary space completely free of internal supports. The entire structure was to be isolated in space, sited in a broad, open plaza.

Despite growing public concern throughout the spring, the archbishop clung to his original choice of architects. Finally, in June 1963, when plans for an uninspired traditional church were made public, Allan Temko, outspoken architectural critic of the *San Francisco Chronicle*, published a trenchant article on the whole affair. "The Cathedral should, and can, be a great building in every sense of greatness, if only the Church and the city together make the best of the opportunity," he wrote. The immensity of the challenge should not be underestimated, he continued, citing as examples St. Paul's in London, St. Peter's in Rome, and Notre Dame in Paris: "A great work of religious architecture, like St. Paul's, must be of its own time, yet ultimately timeless. It must belong to its own people and place, but also to the world." In short, Temko bluntly questioned whether the selection of architects should be left to the church, given the importance of the building to the city at large.

Faced with mounting criticism, Archbishop McGucken spoke with Father Godfrey Diekmann from St. John's Benedictine Abbey in Minnesota who had been involved in commissioning Marcel Breuer for the abbey church there. Diekmann knew of Belluschi, as he had been one of the thirteen or so architects they had considered before selecting Breuer. At Diekmann's suggestion, the archbishop also consulted Father Illtud Evans, an English Dominican who was in California lecturing on modern Catholic architecture. Of the several names Diekmann sug-

gested, the archbishop found Belluschi the most interesting—a Roman Catholic by birth, the dean of architecture and urban planning at MIT, an experienced church designer, and, most important, a man with a worldwide reputation. Diekmann also suggested Nervi, who had been the structural engineer at St. John's. As a result of these discussions, in July 1963 Belluschi was asked to serve as design consultant, with Nervi as structural consultant, to work in association with the local firm of McSweeney, Ryan & Lee. Over the next several years, with Belluschi in Cambridge, Nervi in Rome, and McSweeney, Ryan & Lee in San Francisco, the team worked out a final solution.

One of Belluschi's principal concerns was scale, how to meet the demand for a monumental building without overwhelming the largely domestic, late nineteenth-century, Victorian fabric of the city. He also wanted the interior, despite the cathedral's great size, to convey a sense of mystery, with an inspiring, yet quiet, meditative space he felt was the essence of the church.

The engineering problems presented by Belluschi's highly complex, structurally innovative proposal were formidable. Compounding these was the site, high on a hill overlooking the city and close to two major earthquake faults. The biggest challenge, however, was translating Belluschi's concept of a vault of warped surfaces rising from a square plan into actual structural form. As neither he nor Nervi, nor anybody in the Bay Area, had had experience with hyperbolic paraboloids, they were treading on unfamiliar ground. Working with his assistant Robert Brannen in Catalano's Cambridge office, Belluschi devised a string model, which he and the archbishop took to Rome for their first meeting with Nervi in the fall of 1963.

That meeting coincided with the second session of the Vatican Council, which was involved in the issue of liturgical reform. The

project, and late that fall Belluschi's scheme was approved. The building would not only offer the opportunity to explore hyperbolic paraboloids and the challenge of doing so in a seismically unstable area, but it would be the first cathedral in the United States designed to meet the new liturgical demands.

After months of intense study and the construction of a 15-foot-high concrete model in Nervi's laboratory in Bergamo, Italy; additional seismic testing and stress analyses at laboratories at the University of California, Berkeley, and Stanford University; plus long negotiations with the City of San Francisco to obtain the necessary variances, the team finally arrived at a workable solution. The final design called for a post-tensioned structure, with the weight of the great vaults funneled onto four massive pylons at the corners of the square plan, each 14 feet across at the widest point. These monumental, sculptural forms, seemingly far too small at their narrowest points, where they meet the lower vaults, to bear the entire weight of the vault overhead, appear massive when seen silhouetted against the corner windows and experienced close up. The vaults, springing from the four great piers and spanning 140 feet in each direction at their base, rise in two stages, first to a square opening 60 feet above the floor, and from there, the four principal hyperbolic paraboloids, composed of Nervi's individual precast diamond-shaped units, soar upward, twisting as they rise, joined at each side and the top by a narrow panel of stained glass 6 feet wide and 130 feet high. Counteracting the thrust of the two-stage, 140-foot-high parabolic vaults are the four great pylons, tied together below grade with steel cables.

The interior, just over 200 feet square, unites the traditional elements of the church—nave, sanctuary, transepts, baptistry, and narthex—in one immense column-free space. The raised chancel, defined by a simple, elegant rosewood screen forming a dramatic backdrop for the pure white marble altar, is located directly opposite the main portal; seats fan out on three sides, so that none of the twenty-four hundred worshipers is more than 100 feet from the altar. The organ, with its cluster of nearly five thousand exposed pipes, is poised on its own sculpted pedestal to one side. The sacristy, a parish hall, meeting rooms, a kitchen, a small museum, and an area for covered parking are located on the floor below, forming a substructure for the

council's chief concern was to broaden the popular appeal of the church by reinstituting a full and active participation of all members of the congregation in the eucharistic service. This uniting of clergy and laity in common worship entailed the dramatic rethinking of the traditional longitudinal nave, with its axial focus and separation of choir and nave, in favor of a space that both symbolized and facilitated a more communal endeavor.

The council's decision in the fall to mandate the reforms was timely. Although Archbishop McGucken had been initially enthusiastic about Belluschi's proposal, he had had misgivings about its radical nature, which he thought too bold for conservative donors. In light of his reservations, Belluschi had prepared several traditional proposals as alternatives. The decree of the Vatican Council, however, was a clear endorsement of the centralized solution. The archbishop was convinced by the decree and by Nervi's unmistakable excitement over the

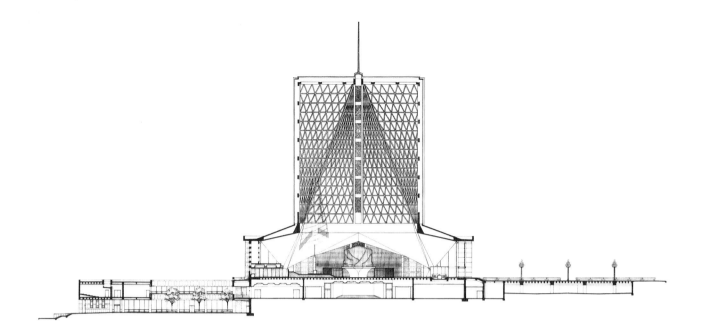

cathedral. Connected to the cathedral below grade, so as not to compete visually, are a high school, convent, and rectory on the south side of the site.

The cathedral stands alone on the crest of the hill, isolated by the uninterrupted space of a broad plaza. From here, one can grasp at a glance the entire form of the building and the full sweep of its high vaults, with the view of the city beyond. The structure is sheathed in white Italian travertine, with darker striations articulating the warping of the surfaces and adding a patterned texture to the building at its base. Low, wide stairs lead to the main entrance on the north and its great bronze doors.

The interior is lit by large expanses of glass, which alternate with screened panels forming chapels on the peripheral walls. The clearly non-loadbearing walls, tinted just enough to cut glare without obscuring views, function as a screen only, with all structural loads borne solely by the four great piers. The effect thus is one of a poised, hovering dome, sheltering space rather than enclosing it—like Philip Johnson's recently completed Roofless Church in New Harmony, Indiana, but now on a grand and monumental scale. Casting a soft, colored light across the patterned surface of the great vault and emphasizing its towering height is the stained-glass cross; each arm extends from the base of the vault, 60 feet above the sanctuary, to its summit 130 feet over-

head. The awesome effect of the highly dramatic space is created solely by the structural forms—the clean, simple lines of the massive sculptural pylons; the swelling, angled arches of the lower vaults of the sanctuary; the rich texture of the coffers in the soaring vaults above, which twist as they rise from square base to Greek cross at right angles overhead. A potential acoustical problem created by the large expanses of hard, reflective surfaces was solved with the help of local acoustical engineers who fit hand-cut panels of acoustical tiles inside nearly seventeen hundred of the diamond-shaped coffers.

Art added warmth and color to the cold, bare concrete surfaces. Belluschi had envisioned the cathedral project as an unprecedented opportunity to draw on the finest artistic talent of the time in a collective endeavor comparable to the magnificent cathedrals of the past. "Artists are the antennas of any given age, responding and interpreting at various levels of competence the spirit which moves it," Belluschi wrote the archbishop in persuading him to secure reputable contemporary artists. "It is my hope that from a passionate dialog between a serious artist willing to listen and a great institution, Art can be restored to its greatest role as a moving and eloquent means of communication." Belluschi again called on the well-known artist Gyorgy Kepes, who was head of the Center for Advanced Visual Studies at MIT and a close friend, to design the stained glass. Born in Hungary and, like Belluschi,

trained in Europe before emigrating to the United States, Kepes held artistic values similar to Belluschi's. A painter and photographer foremost, Kepes was concerned with light and color. Although the archbishop had requested traditional representational art, Kepes proposed instead abstract panels of faceted glass that would funnel colored light into the depths of the great vault. Composed of small, 1-inch-thick pieces of chipped colored glass, each panel had a predominant color—blue, green, red, or yellow, symbolizing sky, earth, fire, and water. Kepes's aim, as he told the archbishop, was "to achieve a clear total unity—an orchestration of the inner space with color." The New York artist Richard Lippold, whose work at the Portsmouth Abbey Church Belluschi had greatly admired (no. 13), designed the great, shimmering baldachino of thin aluminum rods forming the centerpiece of the church. Shooting reflected rays of colored light from the stained glass above onto the polished white marble altar below, it was climactic, a contemporary version of Bernini's baldachino at St. Peter's in Rome.

From the moment the radical design was revealed until completion seven years later, however, the building was controversial. A magnet for some of the most wrenching social and political battles of the 1960s, it was attacked on all fronts—that the money spent ought instead go to the poor, that the land it was built on should be given over for public use, that its forms were elitist rather than popular in appeal.

Architectural critics were equally harsh. The proportions of the exterior came under particular attack, compromised as they were by programmatic as well as technical requirements. Originally the vaults were to have been a third higher and rise in a single, unbroken sweep, rather than in two stages; the requirement of twenty-four hundred seats called for a broader base than Belluschi had wanted; seismic factors necessitated a higher base than he had envisioned; and both cost and the scale of the city's architecture limited the vault's overall height.

There were other problems. The handling of the base was never fully resolved. Thomas Creighton, a former editor of *Progressive Architecture* and a member of a design review committee of the San Francisco Redevelopment Agency, under whose jurisdiction the project had fallen, had urged that the base be fully glazed to reveal the four structural supports. Belluschi, however, wanted the base screened to reduce the amount of light in the interior. As a result, from the exterior one

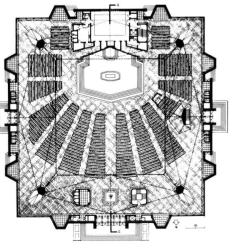

its spiritual function, it is wholly modern in form. Speaking neither to an architectural avant-garde nor to a narrow denominational sect, St. Mary's addresses people of all backgrounds and creeds and is universal in form and meaning. A building that people of all ages understand, it is timeless in appeal.

In 1972 the cathedral was recognized by the Consulting Engineers Council with an honor award for engineering achievement.

REFERENCES

Mies van der Rohe, in "The New Churches." *Time Magazine*, Dec. 26, 1960, 28.

Letters: John Carl Warnecke to Belluschi, Jan. 21, 1963; Belluschi to Warnecke, Feb. 5, 1963 (Belluschi's personal collection).

Temko, Allan. "S.F.'s New Cathedral: A Critical Essay." *San Francisco Chronicle*, June 15, 1963.

"Monumental Cathedral for the Modern Age: Project for San Francisco's New Roman Catholic Cathedral." *Architectural Forum* 120, no. 3 (Mar. 1964): 11.

"Powerful Cathedral for San Francisco." *Progressive Architecture* 45, no. 3 (Mar. 1964): 69.

Letter, Belluschi to Archbishop Joseph T. McGucken, probably early 1965 (Belluschi Collection, George Arents Research Library, Syracuse University).

"Focus: Controversial Cathedral." *Architectural Forum* 131, no. 3 (Oct. 1969): 72.

"Focus: St. Mary's Cathedral." *Architectural Forum* 133, no. 5 (Dec. 1970): 5.

"Sound Control Reaches New Heights." *Form and Function* 2 (1971): 2–5.

"St. Mary's Cathedral, San Francisco." *Architectural Record* 150, no. 3 (Sept. 1971): 113–20.

Adams, Gerald. "The Agony and the Ecstasy." *San Francisco Chronicle*, Oct. 18, 1974.

Hayes, Bartlett. *Tradition Becomes Innovation: Modern Religious Architecture in America* (New York: Pilgrim Press, 1983), pp. 77, 111; figs. 74, 112.

Gaffey, James P. "The Anatomy of Transition: Cathedral-Building and Social Justice in San Francisco, 1962–1971." *Catholic Historical Review* 70, no. 1 (Jan. 1984): 45–77.

Taped interviews, Robert Brannen with author, 1969–90.

Letters and personal communication, Father Geoffrey Diekmann to author, 1990.

cannot see the great piers that support and counter the thrust of the vault, which appears to be perched, like the crown of a hat, on too broad a brim below. The great bronze doors by the Italian sculptor Enrico Manfrini, which Belluschi had hoped would equal the Ghiberti doors in the Florentine Baptistry, also did not live up to his expectations.

Whatever St. Mary's flaws, however, they stemmed less from a lack of vision or failure of spirit, as Mies had predicted, than from the extraordinary demands of the project itself. Multiple worries took their toll on Belluschi: the technical exigencies imposed by the use of hyperbolic paraboloids, the structural complications of building on seismically unstable land, the years of negotiations with the city to get the innovative project approved, and then the construction itself, which was held up for months by protests over poverty, civil rights, and the environment—problems compounded by rapidly rising inflation.

Nonetheless, St. Mary's, based on a highly complex structural concept and realized in simple, clean lines and pure sculptural forms, is an intellectual, technical, and spiritual tour de force, a daring, dramatic departure from traditional cathedral construction. Expressive of

27. ST. MARGARET OF CORTONA CATHOLIC CHURCH

Modest Catholic church outside Columbus, Ohio (1963–70)
Architect: Pietro Belluschi; associates: Brubaker/Brandt; assistant:
Robert Brannen
Cost: $277,949

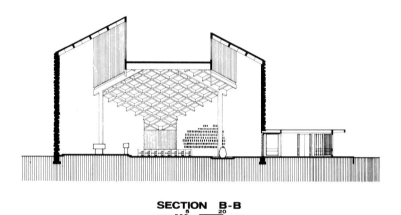

SECTION B-B

Belluschi thoroughly enjoyed this project for a Catholic church because it was for an Italian parish near a quarry, which inspired the use of a form and materials reminiscent of Italian country churches in Tuscany; because he felt a bond with his principal client, Father Kulp, who had been an architectural student before entering the priesthood; and because the job presented a distinct challenge.

The church was for a predominantly Italian community of working-class families, many of whom were descendants of stone quarry laborers from Cortona, Italy, and worked in the Marble Cliff limestone quarries outside Columbus. The existing chapel, built some forty years earlier, was no longer adequate. A new one was to seat three hundred but be capable of accommodating more. The site, on a major thoroughfare, was "not very attractive," in the words of the pastor. The budget for the church, including furnishings, was a meager $200,000.

Originally commissioned in the summer of 1963, after Belluschi had begun the design of St. Mary's, the project was delayed until the spring of 1966. During this time Belluschi's thinking changed, largely as a result of the Vatican Council's mandate on liturgical reform and his continued contact with the ideas of the theologian Paul Tillich.

Like Tillich, Belluschi felt that new symbols needed to be created as faith in the old ones declined, symbols that recalled yet reinterpreted the old ones. Belluschi took Tillich's dictum that the church building itself should serve as symbol to mean that a building should have an

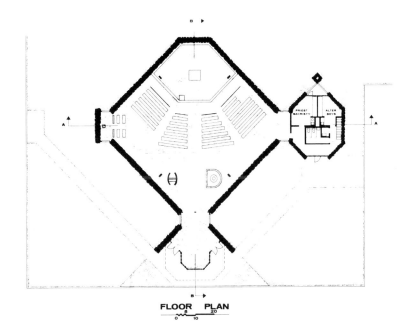

FLOOR PLAN

identifiable, recognizable image, a sculptural form not necessarily large but with presence.

St. Margaret of Cortona consists of a rugged complex of clustered angular forms, with asymmetrical shed roofs and high monitor windows of stained glass held in a wooden grid. These windows cast a wash of natural light down the rough textured walls. The exterior walls are of random stone, quarried and laid by local craftsmen, with wide joints and mortar tinted to match or blend with the hue of the stone. Stones of various sizes and shapes were laid, as Belluschi put it, "in a general but not too mechanical horizontality—just as the masons in the old country put their stones together on general horizontal mortar beds, allowing however for the unevenness of each stone, and without worrying if the mortar joints are quite wide."

Despite its roots in the simple vernacular churches of Tuscany, St. Margaret of Cortona bears clear evidence of the trend in architecture of the early 1960s away from the purism of Mies van der Rohe to a more site-specific, functionally responsive design approach. Rather than following Mies's ideal of a flexible, universal structure, Belluschi here allowed specifically defined functional spaces to determine the overall massing of the building. More specific formal influences include buildings such as Eero Saarinen's Morse and Stiles Colleges at Yale University and the Engineering Science Center at the University of Colorado, for which Belluschi had served as a consultant. But St. Mar-

garet also represents the distillation of Belluschi's thinking about natural light and its ability to modulate interior space. Light and space had always been Belluschi's paramount concerns in church design. These priorities were reaffirmed both by his exposure to Paul Tillich and by his visit to Chartres Cathedral in May 1966, just as the design of St. Margaret of Cortona got underway. The success of a church, Belluschi continued to believe, ultimately lay more in the quality of its space made meaningful by light than in the sculptural character of its exterior.

The Cortona church received an honor award from the National Conference on Religious Architecture in 1970 and a second award from the Architects Society of Ohio in 1971.

REFERENCES

Letters: James Kulp to Belluschi, July 17, 1963; Belluschi to Kulp, May 22, 1967 (Belluschi Collection, George Arents Research Library, Syracuse University).

"July Reports: Thirty-first National Conference on Religious Architecture." *Faith and Form* 3 (Fall 1970): 10–23.

"Focus: Award-winning Church." *Architectural Forum* 134, no. 1 (Jan. – Feb. 1971): 6.

"Saint Margaret of Cortona Church," *Liturgical Arts* 40, no. 1 (Nov. 1971): 32–33.

Letters and personal communication, Leland Brubaker to author, 1990.

28. CHRIST THE KING LUTHERAN CHURCH

Project for a Lutheran church at an inner-city site in Chicago, Illinois (1964)

Architects: joint venture, Pietro Belluschi and Eduardo Catalano

The program called for a relatively small church of approximately 350 seats on a confined, inner-city lot directly on the Chicago Loop. The architects aimed at creating a form that exerted a strong presence, rejecting the reticence associated with Mies van der Rohe in favor of a visually assertive, Le Corbusier–inspired monumentality.

The design, in which Catalano played a major role, consisted of a concrete or masonry building, simple and elemental in form, with a truncated pyramid set on a square base. Fenestration of the exteriors was minimal, consisting mainly of vertically run, narrow, stained-glass panels.

REFERENCES

Taped interviews: Eduardo Catalano with author, Mar. 29, 1989; Robert Brannen with author, Apr. 6 and 11, 1989.

29. TEMPLE B'NAI JESHURUN

Large synagogue for a Reform Jewish congregation in Short Hills, New Jersey (1964–68)
Architects: Pietro Belluschi and Kelly & Gruzen
Cost, including furnishings and landscaping: $3 million

This commission called for a substantial building complex on a tight site amid the heavily wooded, rolling hills of New Jersey. The client was a 118-year-old Reform Jewish congregation, the largest in New Jersey. A new sanctuary was needed with a seating capacity of at least one thousand, plus a social hall seating twelve hundred, a lounge, chapel, library and board room, administrative offices, school, and other facilities.

The synagogue consists of a three-story, L-shaped building with the square sanctuary located in the exterior angle. Eleven hundred people can be seated, five hundred on the main floor and six hundred in the balcony, which, wrapping around the sanctuary on all four sides, increases the seating capacity without destroying the intimate size and volume of the main sanctuary space. Joined to the sanctuary by means

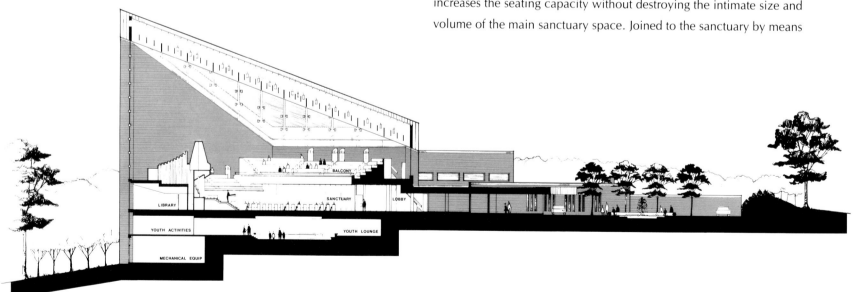

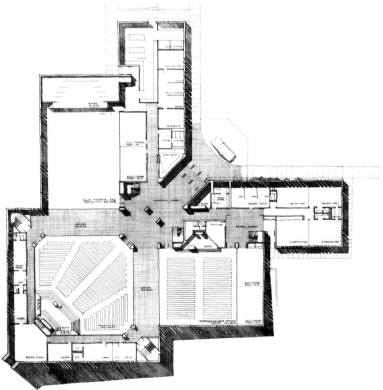

of movable partitions are a 350-seat chapel on one side and an 800-seat social hall on the other, which, when opened up on High Holidays, expand the capacity of the sanctuary to 2,250. Educational facilities, including seventeen classrooms, a library, and student lounge, are located on a lower floor.

The structure is of fireproofed steel, with smooth-faced, reddish brown brick exteriors. Laminated wood beams and steel trusses, exposed on the interior, support the metal roof.

The sanctuary is lit primarily by a slender, 80-foot-high stained-glass panel behind the bema, designed by the artist Jean-Jacques Duval. Its height and light emphasize the spaciousness of the simple, high-arched ceiling of finished wood.

REFERENCES

"A Contemporary Synagogue." *Architecture New Jersey*
    (May–June 1969): 12–13.
Letters, Jordan L. Gruzen to author, Feb.–Mar. 1990.

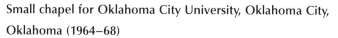 30. BISHOP W. ANGIE SMITH CHAPEL

Small chapel for Oklahoma City University, Oklahoma City, Oklahoma (1964–68)
Architect: Pietro Belluschi; associate: John Reid; assistant: Robert Brannen
Cost: $1 million

Although originally commissioned in 1961, the Bishop W. Angie Smith Chapel project was postponed for fund-raising until 1964, when the design was begun. The program called for a large chapel for the Methodist Oklahoma City University. There was to be seating capacity for one thousand, with the main floor accommodating six to seven hundred and a balcony or transepts furnishing additional seating. The chapel was to provide a place where the campus community could meet for the most sacred of its functions: communal worship. It was hoped the building would also serve as a student center, where groups might meet for fellowship and meetings, and as a place of solitude and meditation for individuals. A private chapel for thirty to forty people, where weddings and other small events could be held, was also required. The site was on campus, between residential and academic areas.

Belluschi originally proposed two very different solutions: an imposing sculptural form sheathed in marble, and a smaller, more intimate one of wood. The final solution assumed the character of the latter. Completed in 1968, the chapel consists of a 650-seat sanctuary with a 75-seat choir. An exposed, freestanding, laminated wood framework on the interior supports a simple, four-sided, folded-slab, polyhedron roof, forming a great canopy over the square sanctuary. Each of the four gables contains a stained-glass window of imported German glass designed by Gyorgy Kepes. A large assembly room, a kitchen, and other subsidiary spaces are on the level below.

31. LUTHERAN CHAPEL AND STUDENT CENTER

Small student chapel and adjoining center adjacent to the University of Pennsylvania campus, Philadelphia, Pennsylvania (1965–68)
Architect: Pietro Belluschi; assistant: Robert Brannen; associates: Alexander Ewing & Associates

The challenges of this commission were the constricted site, extensive program, and limited budget of $300,000. Belluschi was brought in at the beginning to help select the site. Under an agreement with the Philadelphia Redevelopment Authority, a corner lot on 37th and Chestnut streets was chosen, with the portion of 37th fronting the proposed building to be closed off for a pedestrian mall.

The program called for a two-hundred-seat chapel with a choir, the possibility of a balcony for additional seating, a freestanding altar, and a narthex providing a common entrance to the chapel and an adjoining student center. A multipurpose lounge large enough to seat thirty to forty was to be the focal point of the student center; with a fireplace and easy chairs it could serve as a congenial reading room as well as a space for small gatherings. Also required were offices for the pastor and administrators, a kitchen, nursery, music room, and a two-room apartment for a resident guard.

The building was to consist of two separate masses, preferably with the chapel sited toward the rear of the lot, away from the street. Despite the dual purpose of the building, it was agreed that the emphasis should be on the religious function and that the form of the chapel should dominate. Belluschi's design was governed by a philosophy "of an austerity which relies for its impact on the sculptural form of the building." Color was of great importance, as were form and texture, which Belluschi saw as providing the building's strength and integrity. He wanted the structure, small as it was, to be distinctive enough to be easily identifiable at a distance.

Subjected to a number of changes and delays, the project underwent a series of cost-cutting measures. A 1-percent-for-art requirement imposed by the Redevelopment Authority presented a new problem. Faced with a stringent budget and unwilling to settle for something beneath his standards, Belluschi designed the art himself, a simple cross set within an orb, the semi-official symbol of the American Lutheran Church. This was hung on the street-front exterior wall of the chapel, constituting the building's only decor.

REFERENCES

Taped interviews: Alexander Ewing with author, Oct. 3, 1986; Jeffrey Alan Merkel with author, Oct. 4, 1989 (Merkel is the current pastor of the church).

Letter, Belluschi to C. Van R. Bogart, Jr., of Alexander Ewing & Associates, Oct. 20, 1967 (Belluschi Collection, George Arents Research Library, Syracuse University).

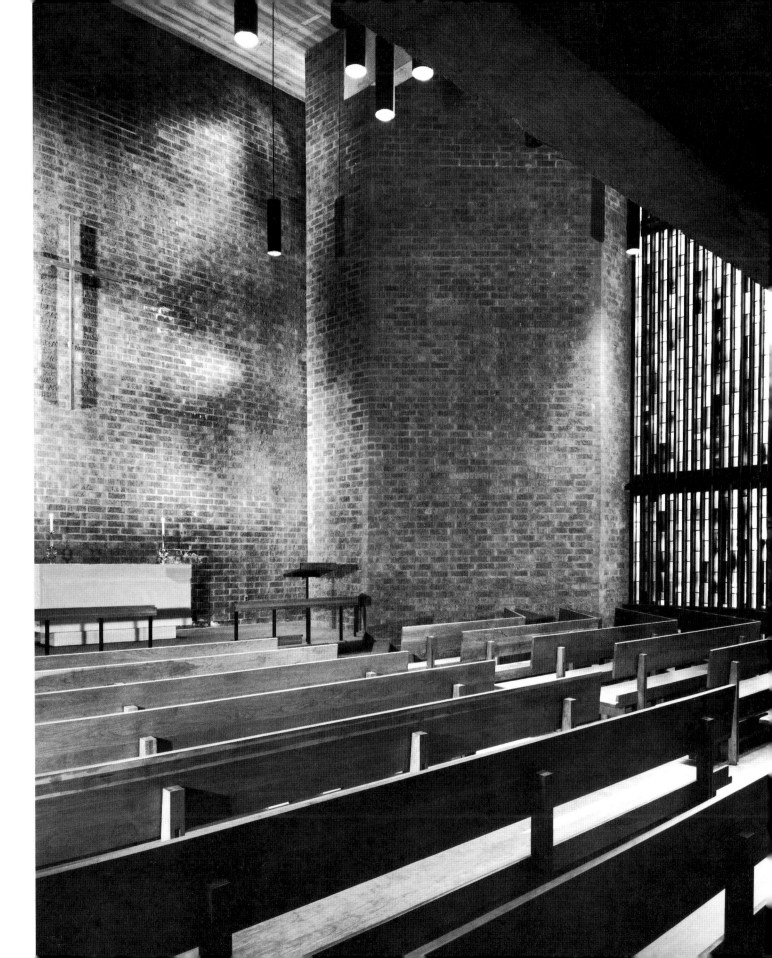

32. IMMANUEL LUTHERAN CHURCH

**Alteration and enlargement of a small Gothic Revival church
in Silverton, Oregon (1966)
Architect: Pietro Belluschi**

In 1966, while he was still living on the East Coast, Belluschi was commissioned to remodel the facade of the 1915 Immanuel Lutheran in Silverton, Oregon, which he had originally expanded in 1947 (no. 7). An entrance for the handicapped was needed, plus additional space for a pastor's office and other service facilities.

Again wanting to preserve as much of the character of the original church as possible, Belluschi doubled the gable to form a narthex, eliminated the stairs, and wedged a nearly ground-level entry and a ramp in the middle.

He was to return to the Silverton Lutheran in 1975 to design a wholly new building (no. 36) after the old one was destroyed by fire.

REFERENCES

Taped interview, Anthony Belluschi with author, 1990 (Belluschi's son, who assisted him on the project).

33. COVENANT PRESBYTERIAN CHURCH

Mid-sized Presbyterian church in Albany, Georgia (1967–72)
Architect: Pietro Belluschi; associate: Robert Brannen;
project architect: Austin Rasco
Cost: $574,700

A new sanctuary with seating capacity of 480 was needed to complete church facilities begun in the 1950s for a Presbyterian congregation. The site was a lovely pine-tree-filled lot facing a small lake in an established suburban area. Site planning was to allow room for future classroom and administration facilities.

Combining some of the ideas explored in St. Mary's Cathedral (no. 26) but now working in wood and on a much smaller scale, Belluschi and his associates devised a simple cruciform, A-frame structure, with vertical panels of stained glass rising its full height. The scheme suggests that Belluschi was familiar with Eduardo Torroja's cruciform timber church project published in the late 1950s. To create a nonhierarchical sanctuary space, the communion table was drawn into the crossing and pews grouped on three sides. The choir is to one side, rather than segregated in a choir loft; the organ is behind the pulpit, the pipes an integral part of the design.

The exteriors are of fieldstone that matches the existing building and stained, rough-sawn pine; the roof is slate. On the interior are exposed, laminated beams, an oiled cedar ceiling, and walls of stone and wood screening.

The church was planned, in Belluschi's customary manner, with a progression of spaces down a covered walkway, through a landscaped court, and into a narthex and nave—a sequence that prepares the visitor emotionally for the quiet, but inspirational, spiritual space inside. The interior is lit by four narrow stained-glass panels that rise the full 42-foot height of each end gable and continue overhead to form a cross-shaped skylight. Each window depicts a different symbol: redemption, faith, hope, and love, in colors that change in brilliance as the light shifts. The glass technique was the same as that used in the Church of the Redeemer (no. 17) and St. Mary's (no. 26), with faceted glass fabricated in the Gabriel Loire studios of Chartres: glass chunks roughly ¾-inch thick were chipped to catch and fragment the light, and set in a thick mortar of tinted epoxy and cement. Lighting the floor of the sanctuary around the periphery are stained-glass windows in screens of redwood mullions. The pulpit, communion table, baptismal font, and organ enclosure are of walnut, each custom designed. The pews were designed by Belluschi.

REFERENCES

Shannon, Margaret. "Creating Beauty in Cedar and Stone." *Atlanta Journal and Constitution Magazine*, Dec. 1972, 6–7, 18–20.

Hayes, Bartlett. *Tradition Becomes Innovation: Modern Religious Architecture in America* (New York: Pilgrim Press, 1983), figs. 73, 93.

Interviews: Robert Brannen with author, Apr. 6, 1989; Austin Rasco with author, 1989–90; Elizabeth Redmond with author, 1989–90 (all are architects who were working in the Brannen office at the time the church was designed).

34. CALVARY CHURCH

Project for a nondenominational church in West Hartford, Connecticut (1967)
Architect: Pietro Belluschi; associate: Robert Brannen

The site was a wooded 2-acre lot in a suburban, residential neighborhood, so steeply sloped that the building had to be terraced. The design went through a number of revisions over the course of several years. The budget was estimated at $461,600. It remained a project only.

REFERENCES
Taped interview, Robert Brannen with author, Apr. 6, 1989.
Letters, Elizabeth S. Redmond to author, May 1990 (Redmond is an architect in the former Brannen office, now with Jung/Brannen Associates, Inc., its successor firm).

35. FORT MYER POST CHAPEL

Replacement of an existing U.S. Army chapel, South Post, Fort Myer, Norfolk, Virginia (1967–71)
Architects: Pietro Belluschi and Johnson & Johnson; assistant: Robert Brannen

The existing chapel on South Post, Fort Myer, was to be demolished in conjunction with the expansion of the Arlington National Cemetery; the chapel needed to be relocated, with its facilities updated. Among the requirements of the job was the approval of the design by the U.S. Army National Capital Planning Commission and the Commission of Fine Arts.

Plans called for a six-hundred-seat interdenominational sanctuary, adjacent one-story administrative offices, and an educational facility. The complex was to be located between the Arlington National Cemetery and a future Fort Myer Community Center, with parking for 285 cars. The budget was originally set at $979,000, later trimmed to $650,000, and then cut again to $625,000, barely enough to cover construction costs of the chapel alone. The educational facility was added later.

The guiding philosophy was established by Belluschi: the building should be recognizable as a place of worship, simple and appropriate to its purpose, in good scale, and free of aesthetic tricks. The church building by its nature should express its moral purpose, he felt, and bear a deeper commitment to an integrity both structural and stylistic than was necessary with other building types. Simplicity in the church, too, was a virtue, as an elemental form would stand a better chance of enduring the test of time than a form designed for novelty.

Belluschi's client proved more conservative than he anticipated, however. In response to the chief of engineers' preference for a structure in the colonial style of the New England church, Belluschi replied that much as he too admired New England churches, they were buildings realized in a different era, facing different cultural conditions, and destined to fill different emotional needs. Were a New England church

to be constructed in Virginia, it would appear contrived, imitative, and inappropriate for the site and times. His proposal, Belluschi argued, conceived in modern times, would reflect not only the specific setting but also the new liturgical trend toward a communal rather than a traditional hierarchical sanctuary space.

The sense of a simple, unified sacred space was to be expressed on the exterior by means of the roof, which was to dominate the form. Materials were to be related to those of adjoining buildings: warm-colored buff brick, stained wood, and slate. Subdued lighting from clerestory windows of darkened bronze glass would enhance the spiritual quality of the sanctuary space.

Belluschi's scheme, although rejected by the Commission of Fine Arts, was eventually adopted. The church consists of a high, four-sided polyhedron roof topped by a slender 60-foot spire, with broad triangular clerestory windows along its lower edge, and poised on a solid, geometric brick and stained-wood base.

REFERENCES

Belluschi, statement on the Fort Myer Post Chapel, June 26, 1968 (Belluschi Collection, George Arents Research Library, Syracuse University).

Letter, Donald S. Johnson, Johnson and Boutin, Architects, to George E. Weber, U.S. Army Corps of Engineers, Oct. 12, 1968 (Belluschi Collection, George Arents Research Library, Syracuse University).

Report to the Federal Planning and Projects Committee, National Planning Commission, June 5, 1969 (Belluschi Collection, George Arents Research Library, Syracuse University).

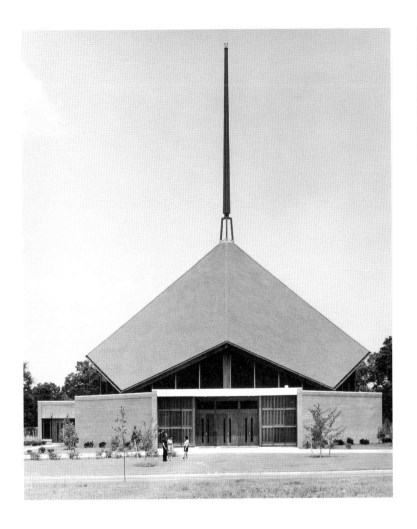

LATE CHURCHES, PACIFIC NORTHWEST

36. IMMANUEL LUTHERAN CHURCH

Small church in the rural town of Silverton, Oregon (1975–79)
Architect: Pietro Belluschi; design assistant: Belluschi/Daskalakis;
associates: Settecase Smith Doss
Cost: $800,000

The first church Belluschi designed in the Pacific Northwest after moving back to Portland was one with which he had had a long history. He had first remodeled the Immanuel Lutheran Church in the mid-1940s (no. 7), enlarged it in 1966 (no. 32), and, when it was destroyed by fire in 1975, Belluschi was asked to build an entirely new church.

The site was that of the original church, at the crest of a small hill above Silverton, in a well-established, wooded, residential neighborhood; the corner lot, defined by two major streets, was hemmed in by homes. The principal challenge lay in providing a modern form that not only embodied the traditional values of the church but also fit the rural character of the town. The project also called for considerably enlarged facilities, with seating capacity for six hundred in the sanctuary.

Belluschi's solution was to place the sanctuary on the main level, with the Sunday school, fellowship hall, and other subsidiary spaces on two levels below. The building consists of a simple, tall, cedar-shingled, polyhedron roof rising from a broad base of cedar siding, the whole surmounted by a slender spire and cross. The main entrance is articulated by a deep, arched, hand-carved portal, which opens into the narthex, then into the nave. The plan is centralized, with the altar drawn into the middle of the sanctuary and the pews radiating around it on three sides. Inspired by the medieval Norwegian stave church, the steeply pitched roof of exposed spruce decking is borne on four soaring laminated Douglas fir bents; these are freestanding at their base with a

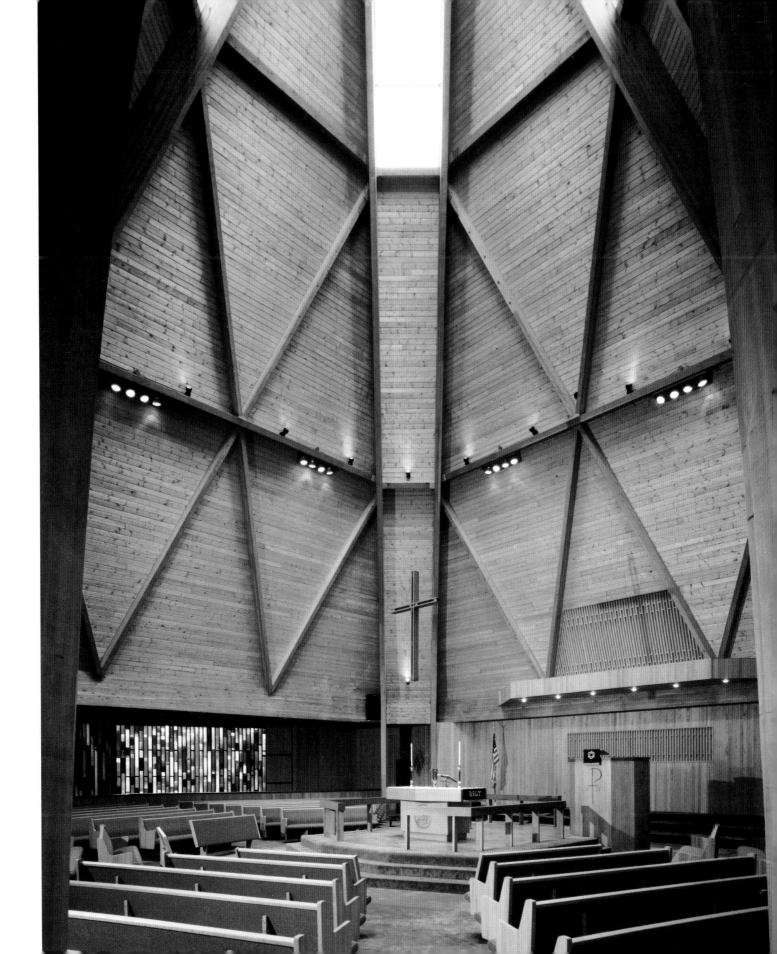

peripheral aisle beyond them, each rising from the four corners to meet overhead. The structural framing is exposed, serving, like Gothic ribbing, both a structural and decorative purpose.

The sanctuary is lit from either side by broad panels of stained glass on the exterior walls, with light filtered into the nave through the peripheral aisle. The main source of light is from overhead, a clear glass skylight in the form of a Greek cross at the summit of the roof which sends a shaft of brilliant natural light onto the altar below. Although the interior is in fact small, it seems spacious, intimate yet inspiring, with its soaring 100-foot-high wooden vault.

One of the most successful interiors of Belluschi's later churches, the Silverton Lutheran evokes the traditional Nordic wooden church, yet it is unmistakably modern in every respect. Controlled by a rigorous structural rationality, with the unadorned expressed structure comprising its form, the building explicitly conveys its function. Aside from the simple cross terminating the spire, and another above the altar, any decoration or symbolism is inherent in the fabric of the building—exposed structural framing, carved portal, and stained glass. Wood carving is by Leroy Setziol.

REFERENCES

Taped interviews: Anthony Belluschi with author, 1990; Phillip Settecase with author, 1990.

37. CHRIST THE KING CATHOLIC CHURCH

Simple modern church for the archdiocese of Portland, in Milwaukie, Oregon (1978–80)
Architect: Pietro Belluschi; associates: Yost/Grube/Hall
Cost: $891,112

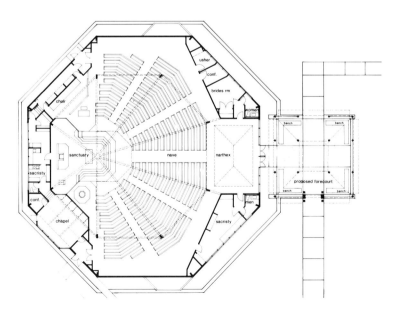

The site of this Catholic church was flat and spacious, in a rural but rapidly growing suburb southeast of Portland. Aiming at conveying a sense of closeness in a relatively large sanctuary space, Belluschi again used the concept of a single unified sanctuary expressed by means of a simple, encompassing, dominant roof form. He adopted a tall pyramidal roof, like that of the Immanuel Lutheran in Silverton (no. 36), but here flattened its pitch and elongated its planes in front to form a shallow narthex. Destined for a Catholic congregation for whom ritual still played an important role, the altar was raised on a dais and drawn into the sanctuary to generate a sense of community.

With an initial budget of $400,000 and a required seating capacity of 650 as his points of departure, Belluschi sought an economic structural system that would in itself convey the desired character of a sacred space. For inspiration he again turned to Nordic prototypes in wood, as he had in the Silverton church, evidently using as a design precedent the Church of the Transfiguration in Kizhi, Karelia, from Hans Jürgen Hansen's *Architecture in Wood* (1971), which he kept by his drafting table as he worked.

Following Belluschi's usual progression of spaces, one enters the church from the north through a trellised gate into a sheltered garden court, which leads to the main portal. Two broad doors of natural wood open onto a simple, shallow narthex, which in turn leads into the nave, an expansive octagonal space vaulted by a soaring, asymmetrical wooden roof. Exposed framing members rise from the walls of the

sanctuary to meet in a great octagonal oculus directly overhead. As in the Karelian church, the nave wall below the springing of the vault is enlivened by a simple continuous arcade wrapping around the entire sanctuary space, reinforcing its sense of unity. Additional light from windows on the outside wall is filtered through the peripheral aisle.

Characteristically, Belluschi relied on the geometric patterning of the exposed structure, the richness of natural woods, the subtlety of differing grains, textures, and color tones, coupled with the orchestration of light and space to create a sacred space—in Paul Tillich's words, a "holy emptiness" devoid of extrinsic ornamentation and relying solely on the eloquence of the void to create spiritual meaning.

Belluschi had originally envisioned as the focal point of the interior a great figurative mural painted on the wall above the altar, like those in the apses of traditional Italian churches. Uncertain of finding an artist in the Portland area capable of such work, Belluschi turned to the known talent of his friend Gyorgy Kepes. Kepes's panel, inspired by one of his works of art in New York which Belluschi had seen and admired, creates the effect of a flickering, starry firmament by means of a multitude of tiny, backlit holes in the wall from which emerges the image of a cross.

Woodcuts depicting the Stations of the Cross along the sides of the sanctuary are by Joachim Grube, Belluschi's associate, a skilled wood-carver and graphic artist as well as an accomplished architect.

REFERENCES
Taped interviews: Gyorgy Kepes with author, Mar. 29, 1989; Joachim Grube with author, 1989–90.

38. UNIVERSITY OF PORTLAND CHAPEL

**Small chapel and student center on the outskirts of
Portland, Oregon (1985–86)
Architect: Pietro Belluschi; associates: Yost/Grube/Hall
Cost, including furnishings: $1.1 million**

In 1979 Belluschi was asked to design a multipurpose building, sacred
in character, that would function equally well as a student center for
the University of Portland, a small private Catholic university north of
the city. The site was a flat, informally landscaped lot in the center of
campus.

The challenge was twofold. The first was to design a distinctly
modern building, fully contemporary in structural technology, materials, form, and expression, that would mesh with the largely Georgian
buildings on the turn-of-the-century campus. The second challenge
was to design a building no different in character from the other secular
buildings on campus yet somehow expressive of its religious function.

Preliminary drawing, Pietro Belluschi.

Belluschi's preliminary proposal, drawn up in late 1979 and using the formal language he had pursued in the mid-1960s, met resistance since it seemed not to fit the regional setting of the Portland campus. His revised proposal, developed in the spring of 1985 and recalling the simpler, more reticent churches of his early Portland years, found a more receptive audience.

Another dilemma Belluschi faced, chronic in church design but especially on college campuses, was balancing a tight budget with the client's requirements. Still more taxing was the problem of reconciling his own aesthetic aim in church design—a carefully orchestrated progression of spaces through rooms of differing dimensions, ceiling heights, and degrees of illumination leading to a dramatic, meditative sanctuary space—with his client's demand for a uniformly lit, multi-purpose building more secular in nature.

The final solution drew upon Belluschi's long experience in church design. The scheme harks back to the 1948 Zion Lutheran (no. 8) in its basic simplicity, simple hipped roofline, unornamented brick exteriors, and interior, exposed, structural framework of natural woods, but bears the influence of Belluschi's other churches and synagogues: the folded-slab roof and glazed cupola of the Portsmouth Abbey Church (no. 13), the slit windows of the Short Hills synagogue (no. 29), the proportions of the sanctuary space and soaring wooden vaults of the Silverton Immanuel Lutheran (no. 36).

Exhibiting a by-now-familiar language, the University of Portland Chapel has unassuming exteriors of rosy brick and cedar, with a broad hipped roof rising over the sanctuary in a low pyramid to a glazed cupola and cross at the apex. A deeply overhanging pitched roof extends over a wide portico, which opens onto a large narthex for informal gatherings. In the center of the narthex is a sunken sculptural baptismal font of concrete in the form of a Greek cross, lit by a flat skylight overhead. Opening onto this informal space are administrative offices, a library, and a reading room. Beyond this lies a great hall, four-square in plan, which serves as the sanctuary.

In a building deliberately avoiding specific allusions to a religious function, all furnishings such as the altar, dais, and pews are removable to ensure complete flexibility; the space can thus be used for dances, performances, or large meetings. Although Belluschi had originally envisioned a large painted mural on the wall behind the altar opposite the entrance, this was rejected as too specifically religious in nature and too directional in its axial focus; instead, a simple removable banner hangs in front of the wall.

The sanctuary is lit from the sides, as in Christ the King (no. 37), by a narrow band of tinted windows around the peripheral wall just below the eaves of the roof. The main source of light is the nearly square oculus overhead, echoing the geometries of the sanctuary itself.

Again, the visual richness was generated wholly by the structural forms and materials themselves. The art, as customary in Belluschi's church design, is an integral part of the architectural form: patterning of the structural elements, stained glass in private chapels to either side of the narthex, richly carved colonnade and portal of the main entrance by the wood-carver Leroy Setziol.

Belluschi's rationality reigns: nothing is arbitrary, everything is carefully reasoned and tightly controlled. He himself considers this the most successful of his later churches. It bespeaks his unceasing quest for enduring quality rather than capricious form.

REFERENCES
Interviews: Joachim Grube with author, 1990; Father Charles Corso, University of Portland, with author, June 1990; Leroy Setziol with author, fall 1990.

39. ST. MATTHEW'S LUTHERAN CHURCH

**Enlarged sanctuary added to an existing church complex
in Beaverton, Oregon, a suburb of Portland (1982–84)
Architect: Pietro Belluschi; associates: Yost/Grube/Hall
Cost: $1.9 million**

Belluschi's principal challenge in this project for a Lutheran church was the site: small, built up, and located in a highly developed commercial area just off a major highway. The client wanted a new sanctuary seating a thousand, plus administrative office spaces, and the adjacent existing church converted into a fellowship hall. A major consideration, then, was relating the new form to the old.

Belluschi's solution called for the use of a bold multidimensional truss fully exposed on the interior of the church. The dictates of this structural system and the building's function, rather than conformity to a traditional church type, determined the church's form. The building is prismatic in shape, with a high-pitched polyhedron vault set on a low base; a projecting portion in the back rises to form a tall, campanile-like tower lit by a slender panel of clear glass. Invisible to the congregation on the interior, this window casts an indirect, natural light onto the altar below.

Belluschi left the exterior plain, saving the emotional impact for the interior. Entering from the parking lot through a landscaped garden, one progresses through a sequence of spaces—garden, narthex, sanctuary—each differentiated by size, ceiling height, and the handling of light. Ornamentation is minimal, with visual interest inherent in the

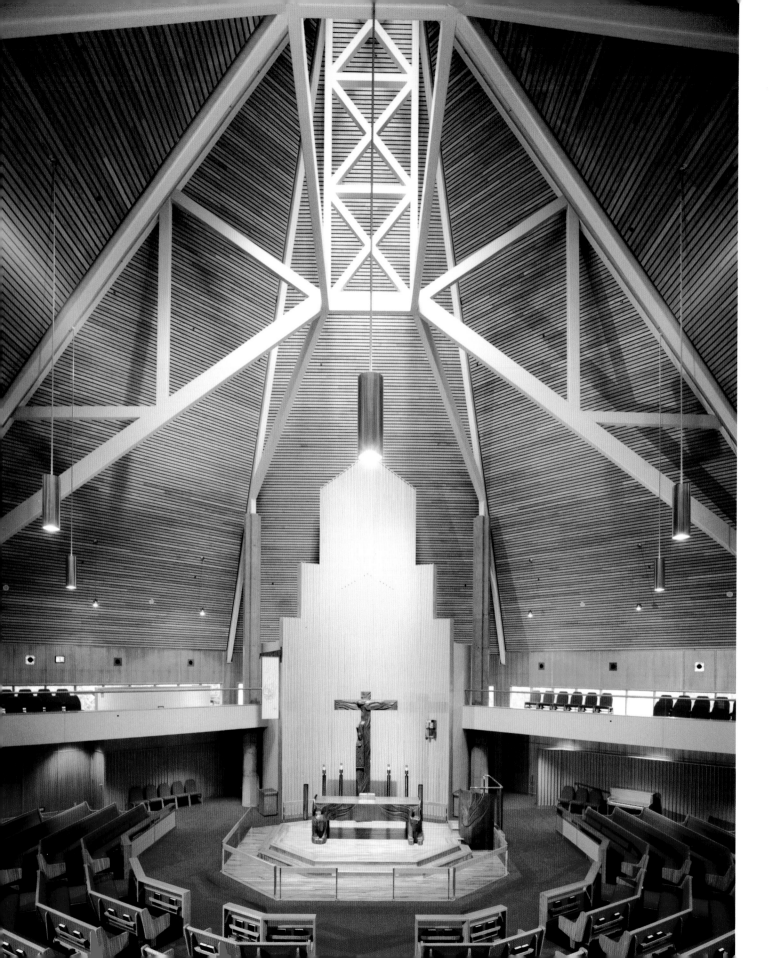

disposition of the varying patterns, textures, and grain of the differing materials—the truss of rectangular steel tubing, the roof of cedar decking, the walls of warm cherry. A simple cross of black walnut from the original church framed by a large, geometric screen provides a backdrop for the altar. Adding the only touch of color and enhancing the warmth of the interior is the rich red carpet.

REFERENCES
Taped interviews, Joachim Grube with author, 1989–90.

173

40. UNITED HEBREW SYNAGOGUE

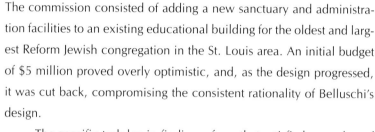

Large Jewish temple in St. Louis, Missouri (1986–89)
Architect: Pietro Belluschi; associates: Stone Marracini
& Patterson; project architect: Robert Barringer
Cost: $5.02 million

The commission consisted of adding a new sanctuary and administration facilities to an existing educational building for the oldest and largest Reform Jewish congregation in the St. Louis area. An initial budget of $5 million proved overly optimistic, and, as the design progressed, it was cut back, compromising the consistent rationality of Belluschi's design.

The specific task lay in finding a form that satisfied a number of conflicting demands. Belluschi wanted the building to convey a sense of the traditional Jewish synagogue without being imitative; he also wished it to recall in a general way the congregation's original 1903 temple, a domed, historicizing, Byzantine building to which the congregation retained an emotional bond; finally, he wanted it to be clearly modern, responsive to and accepting of the values and concerns of the current generation. Wanting this continuity between the contemporary context and the past, Belluschi turned to the 1903 synagogue and the old domed synagogues of Rome for inspiration.

The temple needed both to look like a synagogue as distinct from a church and to relate visually to a ten-year-old, one-story, brick school building on the property. The site was a 15-acre lot of rolling terrain, bounded on one side by a steep ascent, on another by the school building, and on another by a major highway.

Belluschi's solution presented a remarkably efficient plan that provided the requisite eighteen hundred seats with very little unusable space. Originally a balcony on three sides of the sanctuary was planned which would be reached by stairs encased in circular volumes on either side of the sanctuary. The balcony was later limited to the rear of the sanctuary to reduce cost, and the circular forms converted

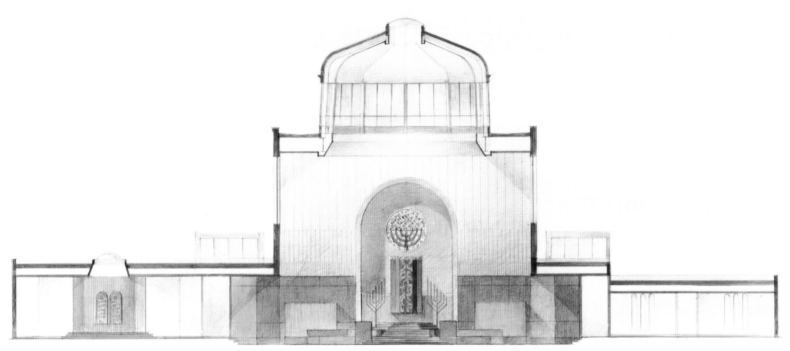

REVISED SECTION LOOKING EAST · ⅛"=1'-0" · FEBR 5 '88
UNITED HEBREW CONGREGATION · ST LOUIS MO · SMP ARCHTS

into display areas for memorabilia. An existing auditorium in the school building is linked to the main sanctuary by removable walls to provide additional seating on High Holidays.

Using a comparable 1927 synagogue in Portland as a specific design precedent (see fig. 49), but stripping it of historicizing features and employing a system of structural steel and non-loadbearing brick instead of stone, Belluschi produced a hierarchy of simple, bold, almost Kahnian geometric forms rising from a broad square base. A 170-seat chapel and administrative offices flank the sanctuary, and a raised twelve-sided dome, or lantern, over the bema in the center are all clearly articulated in separate volumes on the exterior. The sanctuary is lit by the twelve-sided dome overhead.

The exteriors are of warm red brick, the severity of their forms relieved only by rhythmic grouping of tall, narrow, arched windows reminiscent of the Near Eastern mosque. The roof of the dome is metal, bronze in tone to harmonize with the bronze-tinted glass of the windows. In striking contrast to the cool, reticent exteriors, the interiors combine ivory walls and cherry paneling with rich, warmly colored carpeting and stained glass in the north and south walls. Above the bema is a hemlock-paneled barrel vault, with a round stained-glass window framing the ark, a replica of the one belonging to the congregation's 1903 synagogue.

REFERENCES
Progressive Architecture 71, no. 6 (June 1990): 122, illus.
Taped interviews, Merlin E. Lickhalter with author, 1990 (Lickhalter is vice president of Stone Marracini & Patterson, St. Louis).

41. MURRAY HILLS CHRISTIAN CHURCH

Small church in Beaverton, Oregon, a suburb of Portland (1987–89)
Architect: Pietro Belluschi; associates: Yost/Grube/Hall
Cost: $832,000

The site for this church for a Disciples of Christ congregation was a spacious, 4-acre, sloped, wooded lot in a rapidly developing residential neighborhood on the outskirts of Portland. The principal challenge lay in reconciling dreams with reality: fulfilling the congregation's need for a church with a seating capacity of two hundred, a fellowship hall, Sunday school, pastor's office, and other subsidiary spaces, all for less than the cost of a fine house in the Portland area.

The solution was a two-storied complex dominated by a polyhedral roof over the sanctuary; the narthex doubles as a fellowship hall to one side. Joining it is a small chapel for weddings and other special functions. The Sunday school, nursery, administrative offices, and other subsidiary spaces are on a level below.

The building material used was primarily wood: exteriors of stained cedar battens and siding, with roof decking of hemlock, interiors of rich, warm cherry, and the laminated beams of the sanctuary and the truss in the fellowship hall of fir.

Centralized in plan, the sanctuary is lit mainly by a tall lantern serving both as a symbolic cupola and a source of light. Additional light comes from three large triangular stained-glass windows at the base of each side of the vault. The image of a cross indicates the particular importance of the window over the altar. All three windows were designed by Belluschi.

The exposed structural framework, composed primarily of six great laminated bents rising from the corners to meet in a square oculus

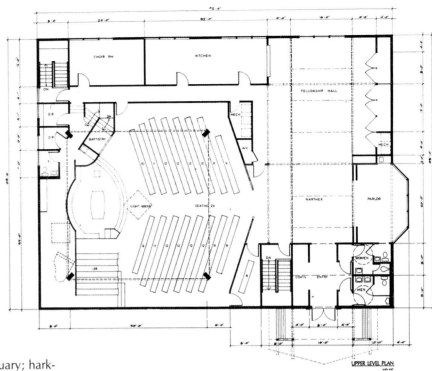

UPPER LEVEL PLAN

overhead, forms a decorative geometric pattern in the sanctuary; harking back to technologically simpler times before laminated wood, a scissor truss, its elements simply bolted together, serves a similar decorative as well as structural function in the fellowship hall. Belluschi's explicit structural rationalism, plus the meticulous craftsmanship and skillful handling of natural materials, lends the otherwise modest building its artistic distinction. The altar cross and stained-glass windows provide the only ornamentation.

Yet another variation on a consistent theme, the Murray Hills church, like the University of Portland Chapel (no. 38), draws on proven prototypes from Belluschi's own past—from the scissor truss of St. Thomas More of 1939 (no. 3) to the vertical massing and polyhedral roofs of his churches of the 1960s. St. Thomas More proved to be the point of departure for much of Belluschi's church design: his Arts and Crafts ideals, simple, unpretentious exteriors, quiet, compelling interior spaces. Like St. Thomas More, the Murray Hills church draws on tradition but is wholly modern in form.

REFERENCES

Taped interviews, Joachim Grube with author, 1990.

42. TRINITY LUTHERAN CHURCH

Small church in Sheridan, Oregon (1987–90)
Architect: Pietro Belluschi; associates: Yost/Grube/Hall

Since the budget for Trinity Lutheran was exceptionally low, Belluschi designed the church so it could be constructed largely by the congregation itself. The site was one block off the main street in the center of the small town of Sheridan, about fifty miles southwest of Portland. Hemmed in on all sides by industrial buildings and conventional small wood-frame houses, the site was flat and without distinction. The congregation needed a replacement for its 1907 white, wooden, Gothic Revival church building. A fellowship hall had been added to it in 1983, to which the new sanctuary was to be joined.

Because the church was to be built by the congregation, its structural system differed from that of Belluschi's other churches. A framework of laminated bents was rejected because it was thought too complicated and costly. Instead, inspired by medieval Nordic examples in Hans Jürgen Hansen's *Architecture in Wood* (1971), Belluschi used a simple post-and-beam system, with wood trusses bolted together by metal connectors to form a decorative pattern.

The exteriors, too, bear a Nordic influence. The steeply pitched polyhedral roof is sloped in two planes, rising steeply over the four-square nave, more gently over the aisles.

As in the Murray Hills church (no. 41), the stained-glass windows were designed by Belluschi, who, in addition to not charging for his services, donated the funds for their execution. Wood carving is by Leroy Setziol.

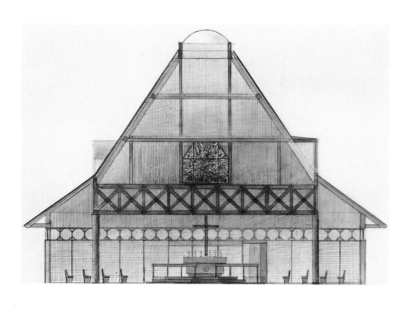

43. CHURCH OF THE RESURRECTION

Project for a small Catholic church in West Linn, Oregon, a suburb of Portland (1989)
Architect: Pietro Belluschi; associate: J. David Richen
Budget: $1.5 million

The commission called for a small church with a seating capacity of 720, on 10 acres of rolling hills in a small, rapidly growing well-to-do suburban community just south of Portland. The program included educational facilities, administrative offices, and a fellowship hall with a kitchen, in addition to the sanctuary.

Using a laminated wood framing, cedar siding, and a shingle roof, Belluschi's scheme called for a fan-shaped sanctuary, with the narthex on axis but the entrance to one side, as was his custom, so that one would proceed through a gate into a secluded garden, then into the narthex, which opens onto the nave.

Belluschi's original proposal called for a raised polygonal lantern above the sanctuary, with a monitor window that would have washed indirect light down the interior wall onto the altar below. Zoning restrictions necessitated reducing the height of the building, which meant eliminating the lantern. A revised scheme called for bubble skylights instead. Because off-site improvements proved too expensive, the site was changed and Belluschi's project did not go ahead.

PRELIMINARY CHURCH PLAN FOR RESURRECTION BUILDING JULY 15 1990
DAVID RICHEN ARCHITECT · PIETRO BELLUSCHI DESIGN ARCHITECT

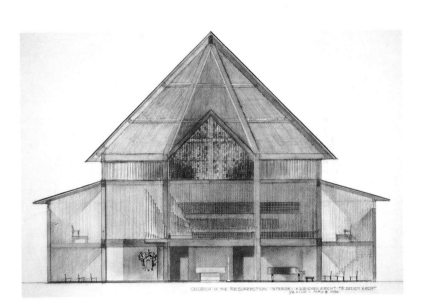

CHURCH OF THE RESURRECTION INTERIOR · Y RICHEN ARCHT · PB DESIGN ARCHT
1/4 = 1'-0 · MAY 8 1990

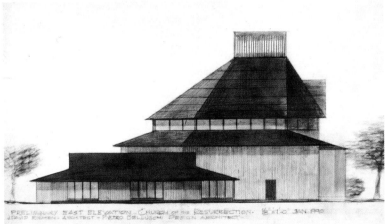

PRELIMINARY EAST ELEVATION · CHURCH OF THE RESURRECTION · 16'-0" JAN 1990
DAVID RICHEN · ARCHITECT · PIETRO BELLUSCHI · DESIGN ARCHITECT

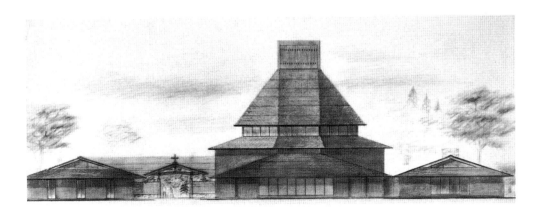

APPENDIX

Selected Essays by Pietro Belluschi

Reproduced as printed, except for obvious typographic or spelling errors.

AN ARCHITECT'S CHALLENGE

Architectural Forum 91 (Dec. 1949): 72

Has contemporary architecture lost the power to create churches that will satisfy the spirit as well as the mind? —Pietro Belluschi

Two centuries of materialistic progress have done great damage to all forms of emotional expression. Painting has had to retract into a sort of individualistic and rebellious introspection; sculpture has lost itself by becoming unrelated to its surrounding; and any endeavor to create purely monumental architecture has become sterile as the stimulus of emotional urgency ceased to be a reality in the lives of men.

After four hundred years of struggle through the sterile and circumscribing influence of the Renaissance and the blind alleys of revivalism, architecture has at last found a certain emotional quality in the drama of scientific progress. What it now lacks in human understanding it makes up in honesty and logic. But the last four or five generations, with very few exceptions, have been incapable of producing works of real monumental character, unless mere size can be accepted as a substitute for spiritual significance.

Of all creative efforts the design of the church is the one which shows most clearly the decay of our spiritual heritage.

Our society believes mainly in the importance of scientific progress, pays only lip service to the old images of God—and finds it difficult to formulate more convincing ones. Our heaven is now on earth; it takes the shape of social security, the thirty-hour week, and restless and uncreative leisure—a heaven, of course, that gives no serenity or spiritual nourishment.

In spite of the advantages and satisfactions accruing to the modern religious congregation by its advocacy of social advances, it must be admitted that to many persons the result of this course is the least rewarding in spiritual satisfaction. To them, God is still an intimate necessity, not satisfied by the knowledge that social advances have been made. To these, and to the many persons who are lonesome and bereaved, to the unhappy people whose only source of courage in their daily tribulations is their opportunity of prayer and emotional release; to the sick and the dying, and the fearful to whom the last source of strength is the image of a personal loving God; to all those, our modern religious establishments have to a large extent failed—and the measure of this failure is shown in the miserable architecture of their churches.

Then what is to be done about church architecture if we cannot find refuge in a sterile copying of the past? Many architects have been baffled and impotent in their struggle to become again simple and believing. Only a handful have succeeded in recreating the atmosphere in which the religious man, the man who still deeply and humbly believes in God, may worship him in appropriate surroundings.

The number of conflicting denominations has tremendously weakened the church as a divinely mandated institution, and the time and wealth which a community can devote to construct its church could not possibly be compared with the wealth devoted to the same purpose in the Middle Ages, when life revolved around the religious institutions. However, if we cannot erect great monuments, we may endeavor to create small temples, in a more human scale, designed in a sensitive and creative manner so as to produce the kind of atmosphere most conducive to worship.

ARCHITECTURE TO-DAY: A SYMPOSIUM

Liturgical Arts 19 (Nov. 1950): 21

I believe the confusion you mention regarding today's architecture stems from deeper causes than a mere question of terms.

In approaching the problem of designing religious buildings, the contemporary architect is confronted by the difficult problem of creating form[s] appropriate to a modern society without destroying the many symbols which have given formal validity to the idea of a *church* in the past. These symbols, crystallized through the centuries, have become identified in the minds of many with religious belief itself, and they give much strength to religious institutions, particularly the Catholic Church. The extent to which we can preserve them and still speak the language of our own time is the real problem confronting us. The modern architect has found that his integrity will prevent him from building with the tools of the past, or to use deception in forcing old architectural forms onto modern materials; yet he has found that he must respect and preserve that feeling of emotional continuity which is the very essence of religion.

You imply that such emotional continuity is provided by good design, but no one can define good design, any more than beauty itself can be defined; all we can say is that beauty acquires full validity only when it is discovered through our own efforts and that its face is forever changing because life itself is forever changing. The efforts of the past we may admire and measure and classify, but we must speak of our own emotions in our own way, because the powers of the human mind draw strength from its own efforts and wilt from imitation. The creative

powers of man are truly a divine gift. It is this creative desire to search for truth, even in a small measure and in his own inadequate way, which stimulates the architect to find new solutions. If he understands the importance of religious symbols as a means to historical continuity, such understanding will guide him and provide the discipline which must always be present in the work of any artistic importance.

From the above point of view, then, the problem facing the contemporary architect is not impossible of solution nor is it peculiar to his day. It is an old one, and each age has met it and solved it in its own way. With all the shortcomings of a materialistic world surrounding us, we too must face and solve it in the full realization that the main function of a church building is to provide emotional fulfillment.

To-day's need for economy makes us avoid pompously designed monuments, but in so doing we have found that much significance can be imparted to simple materials such as wood or brick, and much warmth and feeling may be achieved by the judicious use of such intangibles as space, light, texture, and color. Paintings, sculpture, stained glass, and other decorative arts, if creative and not merely imitative, add immeasurably to the proper solution of the problem which, as I noted before, is to create an environment in which the average man may find spiritual shelter; a place where he may draw strength for his daily labors, and courage in his battle and temptations, a place where he may join others in worship and meditation.

I do not agree with the premise that if the liturgy is understood and appreciated, all other questions are readily solved, because the examples of many churches built in recent decades, while fulfilling all liturgical requirements, have failed to a great extent to create the emotional impact so necessary in the House of God.

I will admit that the task is more easily stated than carried out, due to the simple reason that there are few really creative minds. So I must end with what may seem an apology: the danger to contemporary religious architecture does not come so much from our right to express ourselves in a modern idiom, but from the fact that so few designers have the gift, the integrity, and the discipline to make such an idiom of convincing significance.

THE MODERN CHURCH—OR TRADITIONAL?

New York Times Magazine, Mar. 14, 1954, 14–15, 60

I once heard a wise clergyman say that today's churches, being intended for the people of our times, should be so designed that the people of our times will recognize them and feel that they are being addressed to them. He was thus in effect saying that religion must be dynamic and alive to be acceptable to the modern educated man. If we believe this, then the case for modern architecture in our churches is an easy one to make.

Present-day architecture, having matured under materialistic concepts of progress, has succeeded in its first task of honest and functional simplification; in so doing, it has taught us two great lessons— the fundamental ugliness of structural deception and the ineffectualness of imitation.

But to many people the word "modern" is still synonymous with "barren" and lacking in the spiritual richness, the subtle emotional qualities, which illumined the great styles of the past. They complain that there is no "beauty" in modern architecture, as if beauty were a quality forever embalmed in time rather than forever changing, even as life is changing. They fail to see that the best architects of our age are, in fact, attempting to do just what creative architects of all times have always done, that is, to impart spiritual significance to the forms they are creating, and that it is their way to search for a deeper meaning of beauty.

Perhaps our age is not one of great spiritual awareness. But it is easy to prove by any standard that imitative forms have no power to move, and that only the joyous excitement of new ideas, surging from a deeply felt experience and expressed with poetic clarity in structural honesty, can succeed in giving emotional nourishment.

The modern educated man, religiously inclined, has the right to insist that his commitments to God be made in such an environment.

He may not wish his temple to reach to Heaven, which was the sky to the man of the Middle Ages; he may wish, rather, that it be human in scale, appropriate to the inward search and responsive to true values and to the needs of a complex age. Any attempt to build in a dead, traditional style under the guise of preserving the past may in effect succeed only in destroying the present for the thoughtful and the sensitive.

Of course, there is good and bad modern, as there have always been good and bad architects, and we know that the temper of our times is against greatness. But if we believe, as we must, that the powers of the human mind draw strength from their own creative efforts and wilt from imitation, then it seems better to have tried and failed than to have surrendered to compromise and to the easy expediency of using dead forms. If we dare to be creative, our failures at least will help to show us better ways, but uninspired works will succeed only in deepening our own inadequacies.

In its moments of greatest vitality the Church has never failed to attract the most creative spirits of its time by bidding them to find new ways and a new language to proclaim its glory. The great styles of the past, which were never static, were themselves the result of this search for renewal, this desire to give freshly felt answers to the eternal mystery of man and his God. And that to the modern architect is the only tradition worth following.

THE CHALLENGE OF ST. JOHN'S CATHEDRAL

Architectural Forum 102, no. 5 (May 1955): 62–63

An address by Pietro Belluschi, dean of MIT's School of Architecture and Planning, before the New York chapter of the American Institute of Architects

The architectural professional has now before it the challenge of proving that the Cathedral of St. John the Divine in New York can be successfully finished in the contemporary idiom (*AF* [Dec. 1954]—Ed.).

There has been a great increase in recent years of congregations willing to take the modern architect at his word. I feel, though, that in this particular case the decision of the vestry to consider abandoning traditional forms, even if only for financial reasons, assumes historical importance and the test is more severe and of greater import than any I know of. In effect we are asked to pit in a most direct and intimate way the results of our wisdom, of our knowledge, of our maturity as architects, against a set of forms which have for a thousand years served as the very symbols of human inspiration to worship. Hollow forms when copies, you say, but still speaking with endearing tones to the multitudes, still representing in the eyes of many people the highest expression of religious faith when faith was at its highest.

We are asked in fact to place on even terms the forms developed by our convulsed, unhappy, materialistic society side by side with those which sprang from the very spirit of man in the most spiritual period of his history. Obviously, in this contest we are at a disadvantage. Neither the battlefield nor the weapons nor again the time is of our own choosing, and in spite of recent progress in our architectural thinking, the physical circumstances surrounding our lives have not prepared us to face the test.

I need not point out to you that the visual world which our own society has given us has been to a great extent, and especially in the hinterland, a squalid refuse heap of ugliness, a tangle of poles and telegraph wires, a succession of rusty automobile dumps, of junk yards, and dilapidated shacks, a nightmare of slums and ugly signs. In this unhappy age of speed and pressures the energies of our creative artists have been directed mostly inward; only few of them have set their hands at the impossible task of bringing some semblance of unity and visual order into our lives. They have made only slow, piecemeal progress, but they are particularly shy when asked to impart spiritual significance to buildings of monumental importance.

We have heard people say there is no use regretting the fact that our age will be remembered for contributions to mankind other than spiritual awareness or artistic inventiveness. They say we should be proud that it has advanced in social understanding, that it has attempted to solve the problem of distributing the wealth among its citizens, that it has tried to weld bonds between nations, certainly that it has excelled in scientific and engineering discoveries; by those values and standards they say our nation has become great and powerful. Yet our answer to these arguments is that in spite of them, ours is not a great society, and it will not be one until it has created for itself a more harmonious physical environment; that is, not in isolated instances alone, but everywhere, a more human architecture. It will be great when there will be a fuller flowering of the arts: that is, when man as an individual will have reached the exalted role for which he was predestined.

Is this being too naïve? I am sure many think so. In optimistic moments it might seem that the turbulent era of the pioneer, of the exploiter and of the unscrupulous empire builder is gradually coming to an end and that there are signs appearing in many guises that some day we may reach maturity. The professional magazines of the world are filled with examples of work done here, and students of architecture from everywhere come to our universities. We may detect in many quarters, if we wish to, a rising regard for human values and a greater respect for order and harmony, a thirst on the part of larger and larger groups for visual serenity where they live and work, and a keener appreciation by many people for the creative arts in their infinite variety. Those may be only faint signs but encouraging and important, even if timid and tentative in relation to the whole panorama of what must yet be done.

We may be encouraged, although sometimes I wonder, when we think of the tools we now have to communicate with enormous numbers of people and of the opportunities given us to raise their level of education. Obviously what we need is a large supply of faith—faith that the masses are really capable of growing in awareness and therefore that they are worth saving, faith also that our more creative people will succeed in producing the spiritual symbols which may serve to reflect and illumine our civilization.

If we hold to such faith, then we must find the courage to face all tests which are offered to our generation. But, and this is my most important point, with that courage must also go the good sense to see that what we do, that is, the answers we give, are not the quick or the superficial ones. They must be drawn from the deepest spiritual wealth we possess. I mean they must include the contributions of our most distinguished creative artists; they must be bold in showing what we believe in, as human beings born in a difficult and demanding age; but what we say must be felt and real. Only in such a way we shall be heard. We may fail even then and our age may be judged artistically impotent, but our failures may well become sources of future strength; but if we are false, if we retreat or compromise, we shall find it more and more difficult in future years to speak with our own voice. That is why I believe most important that we delay no longer the search of our own measure, the testing of our poetic and artistic potential.

It was Francis Bacon, I believe, who first proposed a scientific era in which society and matter were to be studied until we finally understood the form of things. He could not have possibly guessed the difficulties which would be encountered by the generations of men living after the industrial and scientific revolutions. But it is still true that art is generated by understanding life and that by such a standard it must be the substance of our culture.

Through many centuries of slow and ebbing progress, mankind has tried with various degrees of success to adjust itself to the complex set of natural and created things which is the world in which he must live. It is a test of maturity on his part to free himself of old forms shaped by other societies, which prevent him from understanding the nature of his own struggle, and to try to grasp the structural unity of his own peculiar world. Only when free and searching will he see and transmit to others the very meaning and spirit of his age; but it takes time and courage and, as I said before, faith to do so.

In recent years we have seen our creative men—our painters, our sculptors, designers and composers—struggling to establish new abstract systems of beauty from which planners and architects may well be inspired to reconcile the practical demands of their calling with new esthetic concepts of form organization. We have seen, in our lifetime, architecture change from a profession serving aristocratic ends to one mainly devoted to democratic endeavors, and with the help of newly developed techniques.

As an art, today it seeks integration, not dominance; it cannot be promoted by unreasonable expenditures; it has set for itself to a greater extent than before the task of transforming and redeeming function—that is, its forms are more than ever rooted in necessity and shaped for a common purpose. Therefore, its work of synthesis is becoming more and more complex, thereby forcing the architect to limit the part which he must play, while needing at the same time greater knowledge as technologist and sociologist and a greater wisdom as an artist. As a creative man and artist, he must be able to sense an ultimate simplicity, a recurring unity behind the infinity of confusing details which is his world. To carry through this work, he must seek and accept the help of many specialists, but his most important collaborators are the sculptors and the painters who will help him as participants in discovery at the very outset of his more important jobs. Together they will find stimulus in the whole range of created things and the power to satisfy human emotions.

So, in closing, I consider St. John the Divine an important challenge to our profession and one not to be taken lightly. If we believe in man's long-range perfectibility and in his power to work his own salvation, we must face problems such as this without a feeling of inferiority, but with the best which is in us. If many people should judge that we failed, it would still be good for us to have tried. We shall certainly fail if we do not summon the courage to come forth with our own or if we fall back, as we must be tempted to do, on compromise and timidity or on superficiality.

THE CHURCHES GO MODERN

Saturday Evening Post, Oct. 4, 1958, 36–39

This is a time of enormous activity in the construction of religious buildings and, likewise, of significant change in church architecture. What has happened, and is happening, should cause no surprise. Church membership has grown from 35 per cent of the 75,000,000 who populated these United States in 1900 to 60 per cent of today's 170,000,000. We will spend close to $1,000,000,000 for new churches this year, and it is estimated that $6,000,000,000 will be devoted to the construction of 70,000 houses of worship during the next ten years.

The gradual transformation of the churches themselves, both as institutions and as buildings, is more interesting than numbers. "Modern," or "contemporary," design has taken hold. One out of every four of the new churches was modern in style prior to 1954. Every other one is modern today. Not a single example of Gothic or Georgian or other traditional design was picked for a top award in recent annual contests of the Church Architectural Guild of America, a private organization composed of architects, craftsmen and clergymen. Every winner was contemporary, and so were the winners among the church entries in the American Institute of Architects' annual honor-awards competition.

Some of these buildings have caused people to say, "But they don't look like churches." In turn, one may ask, "What is a church?" This question is not so simple to answer as it was in our forefathers' time. It leads us to think more about the meaning of religion and the ways it may fill man's need for spiritual guidance in a modern society. With few exceptions, all faiths and denominations have come to feel that they must address themselves to the people in words and deeds related to present-day conditions. They must show the questioning young men and women who have turned to them that religious institutions are not obsolete establishments but lively and sympathetic instruments of spiritual awareness.

To the uprooted and lonely man of the machine age, the church must offer fellowship and something approaching the social intimacies of the old village communities. The new churches tend to be less stately, and they serve smaller congregations. They are not only sanctuaries but also complex meeting places with Sunday schools, auditoriums for plays and dances, social rooms with dating parlors and hi-fi. Some have bowling alleys, table tennis and outdoor tennis courts. Most have kitchens to serve social gatherings. The Wesley Memorial Methodist Church of High Point, North Carolina, has planned for ten bowling alleys, a swimming pool, an ice-skating rink, a gymnasium, three softball diamonds and several tennis courts. This may be an extreme case, but it is true that no active congregation today is satisfied with just a chapel for worship.

The church as a place for social fellowship is a typical American development. It was inevitable that the fulfillment of this and other needs would produce new architectural forms. If some of these forms have so far been disappointing or uninspired, it has been because of the difficulties in finding wise interpreters and the right expressions. Emphasis on social and lay activities in the modern church, for instance, creates a problem which is not always recognized. This is the importance of preserving or even enhancing the over-all emotional content so necessary to a place of worship.

It is helpful that more and more American congregations have become less timid and have been willing to take the modern architect at his word. Building committees are less inclined to say to their architects, "Why change? Why not use traditional style for our new church?" Or "Why not use Gothic, which in many lands, through so many generations and in so many exquisite variations, has given emotional fulfillment to countless people and deepened their act of communal worship?"

If these questions, so apparently logical and sincerely felt, are asked today, the architect is ready with equally logical, if not wholly satisfactory, answers—such as the greater complexities of modern church functions, the high cost of making reasonably good copies of old styles, the disappearance of the old dedicated craftsmen who could fashion the details so much a part of their over-all beauty, the changing techniques of our builders, and the like.

But there are deeper and more compelling reasons for the search for newer forms. These reasons are in the realm of the spirit, in man's search for knowledge of himself, of the universe and of God. This creative urge cannot content itself with pallid imitations or copies of "regurgitated" styles; it must find new ways of expressing itself.

Religion and art are both a search for truth, which is forever eluding, forever challenging, never fully possessed, only intuitively felt, and the very essence of God's mystery. The fruits of this continuous search, when made in earnest and not by repeating worn-out formulas, carry the deepest and most durable meaning through the ages. That is why the church in its glorious past has often been the fountainhead of creative arts—architecture, mosaics, painting, sculpture and music. At other less vital times, it has contented itself with imitation, timidly picking away at the past, afraid to meet the challenge of the future. The nineteenth century, although it had its exceptions, was such a sterile age.

Today the church seems on the threshold of recapturing its traditional role, and artists are called in greater number to aid our architects in their exploration of the true meaning of "church" in a modern world. Many believe that its design must bear an intimate relationship to the congregation for which it is built. The Rev. Hugh Peniston summed up the feeling of pride of his congregation in their new church in Cottage Grove, Oregon, when he wrote in *Presbyterian Life*: "It is different from any other church—but it ought to be. It is built for us—our own community, our own needs, our own faith."

When Mr. Peniston first came to see me, he and his building committee had visited many churches and already knew that their new church need not be ornate, but should have character, should be distinctive and should be built to house *their* program. This, of course, is the same attitude of the man who wants to build a house for his family; it must fit his needs, his taste, his habits, his purse.

Architects today are making sincere efforts to understand the peculiar qualities and demands of their church clients. By using honest means in their churches—and avoiding the over-ornate—they hope to suggest true and lasting values. By using a more human scale—and not just the monumental—they impart to the whole a sense of warmth and security which may inspire its members to a renewed sense of community life. This desire to share religious experience with other people is the very nature and tradition of the church, even though certain activities may appear to be overly mundane.

Once while struggling with the problem of the kitchen for an Episcopal church in Baltimore, I let slip the remark that the kitchen seemed to have become more important than the altar. The rector, the Rev. Bennett Sims, a most enlightened man, put me right by referring me to the Last Supper, which, along with other meanings, is the symbol of the communal experience of bread breaking.

Today's need for economy is another reason why modern architects avoid designing overly ornamented buildings. Thus disciplined, they have discovered that much aesthetic significance can be imparted by the simplest materials used with a keen perception of their natural qualities. Great warmth and feeling likewise can be achieved by the right manipulations of subtle intangibles, such as space, light, color and texture, thus returning to the essential meaning of all architecture, which is "aesthetic manipulation of space."

In sensitive and skilled hands, space creates suspense and drama: the light it receives, with its accents and its shadows gives a hint of mystery and becomes a means to deepen space itself, while texture and color may provide a moving poetic experience. The Holy Cross Chapel in Arizona, by Anshen & Allen, frames through its large altar window the most inspiring view I have ever beheld. Here, nature through design becomes a part of the religious experience. The Christ Lutheran Church in Minneapolis, by Eliel Saarinen, and the First Methodist in Midland, Michigan, by Alden Dow, are examples of superb handling of light and materials.

By inviting all kinds of true artists to participate in the creative act, architects have added immeasurably to the spiritual message which must be conveyed. Emil Frei's large stained-glass window in the Church of St. Ann, in Normandy, Missouri, by architect Joseph Murphy, is a contribution to be remembered.

The designer who keeps in mind the needs of those who worship is apt to avoid the shallows of contemporary irrelevancies and the cheapness of the merely startling, which is the main danger lurking over all experimentation. More importantly, this disciplined and serious approach may provide the tie with the past—the continuity of real tradition—without being forced to rely on imitations of past experiences.

Actually, every style ever developed, including the much-admired, white-spired Colonial church of the New England village, was conceived that way—by tapping the spiritual resources of the citizens for whom it was built. Architecture is, and it always has been, an expression of the human spirit. Church architecture cannot avoid the adventurous path toward self-renewal without decaying, even though the good and the bad may sprout together. The satisfying answers are not alone in the minds of architects and artists, but in the very fabric of our society.

In this respect, the National Council of the Churches of Christ in the U.S.A. has significantly proclaimed that "the task of the church in the area of the arts is to know contemporary culture in all its expressions, to assess and interpret them in terms of Christian criteria and to heal the breach that has arisen between the religious institutions and those chiefly identified with the arts in our society." And it ends by insisting that "the church should have a vanguard of men and women qualified to interpret the significance of contemporary art, architecture, music, literature and criticism for the believer."

When the new chapel for the Air Force Academy in Colorado Springs—a brilliant and forceful contemporary concept—was attacked in Congress, the members of the Commission on Architecture of the National Council of Churches voted unanimously and enthusiastically their approval and support of the design. The *Liturgical Arts*, a Catholic magazine, has for many years and with visible success espoused the cause of contemporary expression. The Lutheran synods have been most active in promoting an intelligent, creative approach, with significant results in all parts of the country.

It is to be hoped, however, that our acceptance of new thoughts in religious architecture be sympathetic, but not blindly so or uncritical. The bizarre, which in our Hollywood-conditioned society usually gets the most attention, should be looked upon with suspicion. The forced, the insincere, the superficial deserve no sympathy; yet we must not go the other way and build only what has been widely accepted for timidity or fear of the new.

It may be well to remember that the word "Gothic" itself first carried a derogatory meaning; it indicated "a barbaric style" imported from the yet uncivilized European north. Yet Gothic, as a bold but deeply sincere effort by twelfth-century monks, won its way and continued to grow and to renew itself as long as the appropriate conditions for its existence were present. When it became just a frozen formula, it lost its vitality and failed to provide the necessary incentive to the creative mind and to the perceptive, educated man.

ELOQUENT SIMPLICITY IN
ARCHITECTURE

Architectural Record, July 1963, 131–35

As I grow older I tend to feel less secure in my powers and more than ever awed by the complexities of architecture as an art of our time.

As I look, listen, and read about the subject, I am rather discouraged by the shallowness of all slogans, by the polished pretenses of historians, but more by the elusiveness of the creative act. Were I to be completely honest, I would simply say to you that I do not know how good design is produced and that the creative act is an agony which cannot be shared.

But, like all architects, I am easily flattered—particularly by the recognition of my preference for those simple qualities which are the basis of all enduring architecture. As you may know, I was asked to make a case for "Simplicity in Church Design." The theme assumes that true, eloquent simplicity will enhance the central drama of worship. But simplicity which avoids dullness is a very difficult quality to achieve, and I find it now even more difficult to define. I am sure though that the simplicity we speak about is not that of the fool but rather that of the saint: the result of deep understanding and purification, or, if you will, of an act which has gone through the fires of passion and reason.

To impart this serene quality, it seems to me an architect should first acquire a certain degree of humility—not in the usual disagreeable meaning of the word, but in its original one of "being of the earth," of partaking of the eternal balance of Nature. He may also be asked that his work be an exercise in intelligent understatement, yet capable of giving an intimation of the mysteries and complexities of the inner life of the spirit.

In other and simpler words, an architect must be able to forget the superficialities which are such a part of all modern architecture, and be willing to open his heart as well as his mind to the faith which animates the religious world.

In my experience, it has become clear that the architect should go slow in imposing his own special taste, no matter how lofty, and should be willing to interpret the special moods of the client. His interpretation can then match the greatness of his vision, if his motives are pure and reflect the intensity of the collective faith of the religious community. In this context, a Unitarian minister for whom I am now designing a church in Syracuse, New York, recently spoke these words: "Our new house of worship needs to enclose us and it needs to free us; it needs to speak specifically to us and it needs to carry us beyond all words and details; it must have our ideas, the smell of our ground, and have grown out of the religion in our soul. Let our doctrines and our forms fit the soul, growing out of it, growing with it. A free people build because they have a need to glorify all their best and most precious insights, they build for remembering, for enhancing, for serving and for dreaming. A free people need to refashion their traditions in fresh new shapes and forms that they may speak vitally again."

In other words, it is the congregation's church, not the architect's church. Yet this fact should be kept in its proper perspective, because it does not mean that an architect must abdicate his duties and prerogatives, but that he must gain special insights. In any case, if he is honest, he will soon find that there are no perfect answers, only questions by earnest men; and it may well be that an earnest quest is the most important element in church design.

Having said this much, I should find myself in difficulty if I tried to describe the ways and means by which eloquent simplicity can be sought. I wonder at times whether all an architect has learned in the span of his career is not more a handicap than a help in designing a church, and whether he is really capable of attaining humility or of shedding the tricks of his trade—particularly those which have helped him give the easy answers to other human problems in other fields. Yet the nonprofessional man who wished to create a place of worship and tried his hand at being humble would have no easy time either, even if his purposes were clear—the Vence Chapel by Matisse being a case in point.

In addition to a valid philosophy of restraint and integrity, a dedicated builder must have an equally dedicated client, able to appreciate and willing to accept the poetic values inherent but not always obvious in simple designs.

The general loss of the natural instincts which is typical of our society, and, as someone remarked, the knack of our technology of arranging the world so that we do not have to experience it, have rendered people less sensitive to subtle values, or rather more vulnerable to the appeal of inadequate ones. So the architect must find within himself the eloquence to explain and to convince, and such a task does not always come easy in a creative temperament which fears compromise and is impatient with the limitations of lay committees and with the general difficulty of defining art. So the burden that the creative person must bear is compounded by his own limitations, which he may

or may not recognize, and by the limitations of the society in which he must operate.

The design of a house of worship, however, comes closer to being pure art, defined as an expression of the human spirit, than almost any other field of architecture, with the possible exception of monuments. In a church practical considerations are important but not paramount; what is paramount is the quality and drama of the space it contains. It is as a visual art, therefore, that church architecture more than other types mirrors a civilization and its religious climate.

Art and religion have been from time immemorial two aspects of the eternal quest to unveil or to interpret the mystery of our existence. The human condition, its fragmentation and agony, the very sense of crisis in our anxious age, are reflected in the works of our artists no less than in the words and acts of our clergy.

The arts in all forms have been the most eloquent means of expressing our beliefs as well as our humanity. Architecture in its long and intimate dialogue with religion has given us a whole series of unforgettable forms. All the historical styles we have known from Assyrian, Egyptian, Greek, Romanesque, Gothic, and so on, developed in great measure from a concern with how best to honor God.

Architecture can be said in fact to be mostly a catalog of symbols, born of religious beliefs, stretching in uninterrupted continuity from the very beginning of human history to fairly recent times. This continuity and the weight of the past have made it difficult for less committed generations to find expressions adequate for their purposes, yet possessing comparable intensity and nobility.

Our own modern movement began as a protest: the men responsible for its development meant to free architecture from forms which seemed to have spent themselves and become hollow. Tradition had become a collection of shells upon the beach of time, from which a noncreative society in a hurry could draw or borrow with impunity. The word beauty itself was comprised by external images of ideas long dead: the obelisk, the Egyptian religious symbol, transmuted into the Washington Monument, finally prostituted into the Minneapolis Foshay Tower; the Greek temple and its perverted image on Wall Street. It took great courage to redefine beauty as an intrinsic quality and not an embalmed image of things past; it took courage to rediscover that tradition, the word so often brandished by building committees, never meant to stand unchanged.

Tradition, in fact, was found to be change, evolution, search. Human affairs have never been stagnant, and architecture in all great societies has had to come to terms with change. It was found that to stand still and copy, or to be awed by past symbols, was to weaken our own spiritual resources and to condemn our creative gifts to impotence—that the present, infinitely challenging, demands the utmost effort from each of us—and that opportunities for thought and action exist all around us.

It would be foolish for me to try to simplify the infinitely complicated human situation. There have been infinite visions of divine power and infinite ways of defining art—all seeking to reveal part of the mystery of life, a reason for their eternal appeal and for their continued renewal. We know that it is in the nature of man ever to probe beyond the boundaries of knowledge. He must forever find new expressions to witness his own deep concern, to forge new words or new meanings for old words, until he finds his own unique revelation of the inner harmony of the universe. However, with his right to fashion his own symbols goes the duty to develop a strong inner discipline.

It is all too easy to delude oneself into thinking of architecture as an exercise in cleverness. There is a real danger that any minor architect may claim the right to innovate without depth or reason. It is essential that our efforts be honest, that innovation be a reflection of inner longings, the result of having found what is central and lasting. Unfortunately, the ways leading to abuse have multiplied with the means placed at our disposal by technology. It is essential for an architect to discriminate and to choose until his work sings with purpose and unity. In the mass of forms and details and techniques at his disposal, he must train himself to eliminate, to refine, to integrate—a discipline which requires long and watchful efforts.

No less than religion at its best, architecture at its best is witness and custodian of the spirit of modern man. Unfortunately, architecture in our culture is so beset by practical demands that only rarely does it succeed in establishing poetic values. Poetry seeks the essence of meaning, so religious architecture must seek the essence of space from which nothing must be allowed to detract. That is why space in a church acquires supreme importance. Tillich calls it "Holy Emptiness." The architect must strive to achieve this quality of holiness. The designer need not become deeply involved in theology, yet he must understand the motives of the religious man; from such understanding he will discover the way to elicit the right emotions in his work.

This, unfortunately, is more easily stated than achieved. It takes great wisdom to say for sure what is permanent and what is transitory, to determine at what stage an architect acquires the right to innovate. Even a great creative mind can be troubled by doubts; yet the great mind will find the courage to stand by his work, if he deeply believes in certain principles which are a part of the common human experience. The Protestant Revolution, for instance, tended to make the church a place for men, not for mysterious rites; but this significant fact was not widely reflected in its architecture until fairly recently. Obviously, the forms of Medieval Christendom were no longer suitable, but it took dedicated men to bring the fact home. At the same time, social forces and advanced techniques were opening new fronts for lay architecture. Function and economy became bywords in a society dedicated to efficiency.

The functional idea, when invoked in church design, was found to be sterile unless it served to emphasize the central moving drama of space. This fact, in the hands of a sensitive designer, opened up infinite possibilities. Simplicity became a foil for poetic inspiration, a deliberate act of restraint, where the excellence of the details glorified the meaning of emptiness. The Medieval enrichment provided by painting, sculpture, and stained glass had already been removed from the temples, because the reformers did not believe man needed carved images in his quest for God; although even Calvin acknowledged that art could fulfill a man's deep-seated need. The modern man is finding that art does not have to describe or intercede; it may exist and flourish in a context of emptiness and silence.

Just as the idea of function has been put to creative use, so the idea of financial economy has forced the designer to seek an equivalent economy of means to define the real substance of space, gaining thereby in insight while avoiding the pomp and vulgarity which is all too often the result of ostentation.

Several years ago at a conference in Minneapolis, I heard the Prof. Joseph Sittler say that the "Community called 'Church'" can know itself to be a community most profoundly when the usual signs and motivations of community are either violently destroyed or authoritatively forbidden. When during the war all the visible phenomena that could sustain, support, and encourage community among Christians were either destroyed or forbidden by law so that there could be no meetings, precisely in that situation this community has asserted its reality and often performed its common task more profoundly and movingly than at any other time. One thinks of the Church of Norway during the occupation, or, as Dr. Tillich reported, of the deeply felt experience of services being conducted in bombed-out tenements in Berlin, or, if you will, the ecstasy felt by the early Christians meeting in community of worship in secret catacombs which were nothing but underground holes. So perhaps the question arises on how a church should strive to express its purpose. A community, but with special aims, it seeks to glorify the spirit or at least to announce its belief in the supremacy of the spirit. Therefore, if it is simple, it must possess the simplicity of poetry. It should intimate and suggest; it should be a segment of space which reminds the worshipper of the infinity from which it was wrested. It shelters the community but it gives a hint of other more satisfying purposes. So its architecture must be a subtle playing of spaces, a preparation for a succession of experiences—through enclosures and manipulation of overhead natural light and through suspense into other spaces and other experiences as movement succeeds movement as in a symphony, with reflective moments of transition, finally reaching a climax of height and light.

Color and light proportions and the quality of the various materials placed in harmonious relationship—and above all scale, the subtlest and the most elusive of all means to bring space in proper rapport and emphasis to the worshipper—are the tools of the professional man. He can obtain strength and eloquence by using them clearly, if not too obviously. Final effectiveness will proceed from the logic of the plan, the clarity of the structure, the directness of means, and from the ease in which even the layman finds his way.

In such manner we may see at work the three great principles that permeate good architecture and in fact all works of art: integrity, proportion, and clarity. It is through them that beauty will shine, not through arbitrary and egotistical ways of catching the eye. This is the inner discipline of which I have been hinting. The work it generates may thus stand as a noble symbol of contemporary man's beliefs. It will reveal to his future descendants the depth of his concern, even the extent of his inadequacies; but it will avoid the frivolities of the tastemakers, who continually demand new fashions, soon to be bored by them, as they think of form-giving as a clever game of skill.

ARCHITECTS AND ARTISTS: INTERPRETING MAN'S SPIRITUAL DREAMS

Faith and Form (Spring–Summer 1979): 8–9

To design a house of worship is in effect to explore our relationship with God and to search for an understanding of the nature of religion as an institution.

When the great Gothic cathedrals were conceived and built in the Dark Middle Ages, religion was the very core of every community. It possessed transcendent powers seldom comprehended in modern times. Religion was then a total commitment of the Spirit. It gave strength and inspiration to mankind, a power which lasted unimpaired for many centuries. The advent of the age of reason filled man with an earthly pride but left them insecure and full of doubt. Ever since, often unknowingly, the Spirit has been yearning for recognition. It is this search for spiritual fulfillment to which I'm alluding when I speak of the nature of religion, though admitting that such a search is also evident in other fields, notably in the arts.

From the beginning of my career I've been intuitively aware of what was demanded of an architect to satisfy this role of interpreter of man's spiritual dreams. Only seldom have I succeeded in my task, but

I felt all along that it was important for me to believe in such a role and to hold firm to certain values leading to excellence. Unfortunately, in a fast changing world it has become very difficult to define excellence. We might be reminded that architects have been trained and exercise their profession in a society where the superficial aspects of things and events are systematically overemphasized. We have learned only too well how to gain immediate attention by frivolous means and how to sell our wares by subtle propaganda. We have done so quite often at the expense of our natural instincts thus becoming less sensitive to lasting values and more vulnerable to inadequate ones. Technology on its part has tended, to some extent, to arrange a world in such a way that it has become difficult to experience it.

Many years ago I attended a lecture by Dr. Sittler in Minneapolis, and I remember being much impressed by what he told us about the religious experience. "The community called church," he said, "knows itself to be a community most profoundly when the usual signs and motivations of community are either violently destroyed or authoritatively forbidden. When during the last World War all the visible phenomena that could sustain, support and encourage community among Christians were either destroyed or forbidden by law, so there could be no meetings, *precisely* in that situation this community has asserted its reality and often performed its common task more profoundly and movingly than at any other time."

Surely the emotions experienced in such encounters were most convincing reflections of man's true relation to his God and best expressing what Paul Tillich has called his ultimate concern. One thinks of the Church of Norway during the occupation; of the deeply felt experience of services being conducted in a bombed-out tenement in Berlin; or if you will the ecstasy felt by the early Christians meeting in community of worship in secret catacombs, which were nothing but forbidding underground holes, visited and well remembered in my youth.

At this point, the central all-important question must arise for an architect: by what means should a church building strive to express its transcendent purpose?

All religious congregations, consciously or unconsciously, seek to glorify the Spirit or at least to announce their belief in the supremacy of the Spirit.

In Syracuse, New York, a young pastor once put the problem clearly to me with the following instructions: "Our house needs to enclose us and it needs to free us; it needs to speak specifically to us and it needs to carry us beyond all words and details; it must have our ideas, the smell of our ground and have grown out of the religion in our souls. Let our doctrines and our forms fit the soul, growing out of it, growing with it. A free people build because they have a need to glorify all their best and their most precious insights; they build for remembering, for enhancing, for serving and for dreaming. A free people need to refashion their tradition in fresh new shapes and forms that they may speak vitally again."

Those eloquent words did suggest to me at the time that my first duty was to gain the special insights which would permit me to go beyond the easy superficialities which are so much a part of our so-called "modern" architecture. Certainly an architect must open his heart and his mind to the faith which animates the religious world and do so with a kind of humility which strives to understand but admits human limitations in the face of the awesome mystery inherent in all truths.

Early in my professional practice, perhaps because of my limited talents, I did find "simplicity" as a philosophy to be a most direct and effective means of enhancing the central drama of worship. But I soon found out that it must be an eloquent simplicity, possessing deeper implications. Like poetry, through the magic of words, it must seek the very meaning of space. Its emptiness must suggest a quality of holiness, precious enough to remind the worshipper of the infinity from which it was wrested; space that is more than a shelter, space that gives a hint of other more satisfying purposes.

The design of a church begins with a structurally convincing volume made meaningful by subtle manipulations of light and shadows, by providing multiple visual experiences through suspense and mystery, through textures and colors, through fine proportions and exploitation of natural materials—all brought together in harmonious relationship.

The most important yet the most elusive element to bring space in proper rapport with the worshipper is "scale." Scale is the most subtle and difficult of all tools to achieve the desired effect on the worshipper. The grandeur of the medieval cathedral was overwhelming; the intimacy of the New England white churches brought God and His word closer to him.

The serious professional man must learn to use this undefinable tool; he will achieve strength and beauty by using it with clarity and daring. Of course, it goes without saying that he must also observe all the many practical demands essential to carrying out the project. The Catholic liturgy underwent sharp changes, which in turn generated new forms. The congregation was asked in effect to participate in the services rather than to be observers at the end of a long nave with the altar behind the chancel. The altar became the visual focus, not the locus, for mysterious happenings. So the space became fan-shaped or square rather than oblong, St. Mary's Cathedral being the first important example of such a plan. It was conceived soon after Pope John came to the Vatican.

The generalities I have just briefly described are distillations of my own experience acquired through the years and are fairly obvious. Unfortunately, it's not easy to give form and substance to one's ideals. We know that through the ages there has been an accumulation of countless idiomatic forms which have hindered rather than helped the architect's task. Within our own time, we have seen forms once fashionable quickly lose their freshness and, sad to say, professional magazines have been instrumental in spreading a vocabulary of tricks, fashions and banalities. In my own practice, I have not been immune from their influence; but what saved me mostly, I'd like to believe, has been the fact that whenever possible I've sought the collaboration of the most imaginative artists I could find. I knew that one single good work of art could redeem a mediocre piece of architecture through its liberating role and I found it to be indeed a test of the institution as much as it is a test for the contemporary artist to find the power and the grace to search for divine truth in all its infinite aspects. In one of my addresses, given almost a generation ago, I said that art and religion have

been from time immemorial two aspects of our eternal quest to unveil or to interpret the mystery of our existence. The human condition, its fragmentation and agony, the very sense of crisis in our anxious age are reflected in the works of our best artists, no less than in the words and acts of our clergy. Father Couturier, the Dominican friar responsible for the great works of art in the church in Notre Dame of Assy, in describing his experience in gathering so many famous artists for that project, did admit that great artists are few and we should take them wherever we can find them, as it is better to turn to geniuses without faith than to believers without talent. He was also quoting Saint Augustine, who had said, "Many are outside the church who believe themselves to be inside, and many are within who believe themselves to be without." In the true artist, the secret and persistent sources of religious faith never fully disappear or deteriorate; they are still the most precious part of his unconscious on which his imagination feeds. He quoted Matisse telling Picasso, "You well know that what we all strive to recapture in our art is the atmosphere of our first communion."

We cannot explain in a rational way the works of great artists, but they seem naturally directed towards the Holiness of the Spirit by whatever name.

But here I'm tempted to express my personal fear that art today might be in deep crisis, making it very difficult to recognize greatness. I will accept that fact that Art, as Dr. Newport pointed out in his address, has recently been nourished in many ways by Science. But I cannot help feeling that when it is totally removed from human conditions and passions, it tends to become shallow and spiritually sterile. So, an architect must suffer the uncertainties of his time in addition to the difficulties of conveying his thoughts and doubts to the client.

There is also the fear of having to compromise just to please his client—the burden being compounded by his own limitations, which he may or may not recognize, and by the manifold prejudices of his age.

Let me end these brief confessions by saying that as there have been infinite visions of divine power, so there have been infinite ways of defining art or of creating meaningful architecture, which is the reason for their eternal appeal and continued renewal. The important thing is to recognize the problem as well as to recognize our own limitations. It is of some consolation to reflect that it is man's nature forever to search for new expressions in order to witness, though in imperfect ways, his own unique revelation of God and the mystery of his existence on earth.

Here then is the real test of our worth—the ability to recognize true values from transitory ones in the light of our perceptions. It is all too easy to delude ourselves into thinking that all changes are equally desirable or into seeing architecture as an exercise in cleverness. I believe it is not enough just to innovate, but it is important that our efforts be thorough and honest, that innovation be a reflection of deep understanding and inner longings, the result of having found what is central and lasting; or we will be swamped by the tastemakers, who continually demand new fashions soon to be bored by them.

Such are my perplexities and in a way a resume of my lifelong doubts of which I spoke at the outset. Wisdom is supposed to be one of the virtues of old age, but all one learns really is that its acquisition is beyond the grasp of the average mortal.

SELECTED BIBLIOGRAPHY

Bittermann, Eleanor. *Art in Modern Architecture*. New York: Reinhold Publishing, 1952.

Church Architecture: The Shape of Reform. Proceedings of a meeting on church architecture conducted by The Liturgical Conference, Feb. 23–25, 1965, in Cleveland, Ohio. Washington, D.C.: The Liturgical Conference, 1965.

Christ-Janer, Albert, and Mary Mix Foley. *Modern Church Architecture: A Guide to the Form and Spirit of Twentieth-Century Religious Buildings*. New York: McGraw-Hill, 1962.

Clausen, Meredith L. "Transparent Structure: Belluschi Churches of the 1950s." *Faith and Form* 24 (Fall 1990): 10–14.

Gubitosi, Camillo, and Alberto Izzo. *Pietro Belluschi: Edifici e progetti, 1932–73*. Exh. cat. Rome: Officina Edizioni, 1974.

Graham, Aelred. *Zen Catholicism*. New York: Harcourt, Brace & World, 1963.

Hammond, Peter. *Liturgy and Architecture*. New York: Columbia University Press, 1961.

Hartshorne, Charles, and Creighton Peden. *Whitehead's View of Reality*. New York: Pilgrim Press, 1981.

Hayes, Bartlett. *Tradition Becomes Innovation: Modern Religious Architecture in America*. New York: Pilgrim Press, 1983.

Lacey, Michael J. *Religion and Twentieth-Century American Intellectual Life*. Cambridge, England: Woodrow Wilson International Center for Scholars and Cambridge University Press, 1989.

Martin, James Alfred, Jr. *Beauty and Holiness: The Dialogue between Aesthetics and Religion*. Princeton, N.J.: Princeton University Press, 1990.

Northrop, F. S. C. *The Meeting of East and West: An Inquiry Concerning World Understanding*. New York: Macmillan Publishing, 1946.

Recent American Synagogue Architecture. Exh. cat. New York: The Jewish Museum, 1963.

Sövik, Edward A. *Architecture for Worship*. Minneapolis: Augsburg Publishing, 1973.

Stubblebine, Jo, ed. *The Northwest Architecture of Pietro Belluschi*. New York: F. W. Dodge Corporation, 1953.

Thiry, Paul, Richard M. Bennett, and Henry L. Kamphoefner. *Churches and Temples*. New York: Reinhold Publishing, 1953.

Tillich, Paul. *On Art and Architecture*. Ed. John Dillenberger and Jane Dillenberger. New York: Crossroad Publishing Co., 1987.

Turner, Harold W. *From Temple to Meeting House: The Phenomenology and Theology of Places of Worship*. The Hague: Mouton Publishers, 1979.

Watkin, William W. *Planning and Building the Modern Church*. New York: F. W. Dodge Corporation, 1951.

White, James F. *Protestant Worship and Church Architecture*. New York: Oxford University Press, 1964.

Whitehead, Alfred North. *Dialogues of Alfred North Whitehead*. Westport, Conn.: Greenwood Press, 1954.

Wuthnow, Robert. *The Restructuring of American Religion: Society and Faith since World War II*. Princeton, N.J.: Princeton University Press, 1988.

INDEX

Boldface numbers indicate illustrations.

PHOTO CREDITS

The author and publisher are grateful to the following photographers and others who provided illustrations. Special thanks are due to Pietro Belluschi for the loan of many photographs. As most of these lack attributions, we apologize to the photographers whose authorship is unacknowledged.

Gil Amiaga, pp.146, 147; Morley Baer, front jacket, fig. 45, pp.127, 128 lower left, 131, 133,134; Andrew Barada, p. 82; Courtesy Pietro Belluschi, figs. 2, 3, 5, 14, 18, 37, 42, 50, pp. 47, 50, 56 upper left, 62, 64, 66 upper and lower left, 68, 69 right, 71, 112, 113, 143, 145, 152–53, 155, 174; Courtesy Brubaker/Brandt, pp. 116, 117 upper left and right; M. L. Clausen, figs. 4, 19, 28, 29, 32–36, 49, pp. 46, 55, 66 upper right, 69 left, 74, 80, 85, 86, 89, 94, 96 upper, 97, 100 lower right, 105 lower, 107, 110, 111 upper, 135, 163, 169 upper right, 178, 182; Columbia Commercial Studio, Portland (courtesy Finley Sunset Park), fig. 1, pp. 43, 45 left; James Coyne, Blackstar Publishing Co., fig. 25; Leonard Delano, p. 52; J. E. Durrell, Jr., pp. 137, 140; John Ebstel, fig. 40; ESTO Photographics, fig. 41; Courtesy The Frank Lloyd Wright Foundation, fig. 39; Courtesy George Arents Research Library, Syracuse University, fig. 6, p. 58 upper; George Miles Ryan Studios, Inc., fig. 15; Gorchev and Gorchev, p.157; Courtesy The Grutzen Partnership, p. 144; Hedrich-Blessing, fig. 10, pp. 119–23; Herrlin Studio, Barrington, Ill., p. 125; Ed Hershberger, fig. 46, pp. 160–62, 165, 167–69 lower, 172, 179, 180, 183; Lawrence Hudetz, fig. 11, pp. 56 upper right and lower, 63, 65, 164, 173, 184, 185; Erven Jourdan (courtesy Finley Sunset Park), p. 44; Courtesy Jung/Brannen, p. 154; Phokion Karas, pp. 150, 151; A. F. Kersting, fig. 30; G. E. Kidder-Smith, figs. 24, 48, pp. 81, 84 right, 124; Joseph Molitor, pp. 79, 83, 84 left, 87, 90, 93, 96 lower, 104, 105 upper, 109, 115; Charles R. Moor, back jacket (middle), pp. 138, 139; Courtesy Oregon Historical Society, pp. 60, 117 lower; Warren Reynolds, Infinity, Inc., fig. 23; K. E. Richardson, back jacket (left), frontispiece, pp. 49, 61; Len Rosenberg, p. 111 lower; Courtesy William Schuppel, p. 130; Julius Shulman, back jacket (right), p. 73; Jack Sidener, pp. 51, 70, 126; Courtesy Stone Marracini & Patterson, pp. 175, 176; Roger Sturtevant (courtesy Elizabeth K. Thompson), fig. 16; Courtesy Elizabeth K. Thompson, p. 58 lower; Sten Vilson, fig. 12; M. E. Warren, pp. 95, 100 upper right; Michael Wurth, pp. 148, 149; Courtesy Yost/Grube/Hall, fig. 47; Courtesy Zion Lutheran Church, p. 59

Illustrations were reproduced from the following publications with the kind permission of the publishers.

Architectural Forum, fig. 27; Jean Bony, *French Gothic Architecture* (University of California Press), fig. 38; E. Catalano, *Structures of Warped Surfaces* (North Carolina State University), fig. 43, p. 128 upper right; Albert Christ-Janer and Mary Mix Foley, *Modern Church Architecture* (McGraw-Hill), figs. 21, 22; Jiro Harada, *The Lesson of Japanese Architecture* (The Studio Ltd.), fig. 17; *Progressive Architecture*, fig. 9, pp. 53, 54; Antonin Raymond, *Architectural Details* (Architectural Book Publishing), fig. 8; Antonin Raymond, *Antonin Raymond: An Autobiography* (Charles E. Tuttle Co.), figs. 7, 13